CONTRARY TO POPULAR BELIEF

COLD
CALLING
DOES WORK!

VOLUME I EFFECTIVENESS, THE ART OF APPOINTMENT MAKING

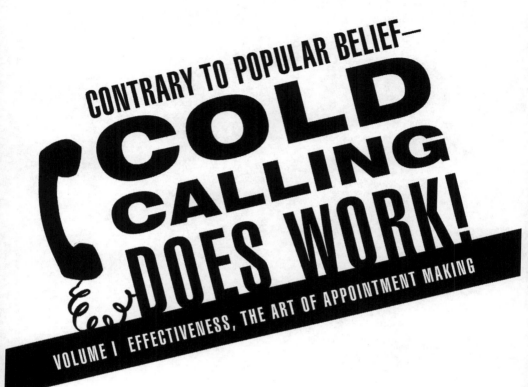

CONTRARY TO POPULAR BELIEF—
COLD
CALLING
DOES WORK!

VOLUME I EFFECTIVENESS, THE ART OF APPOINTMENT MAKING

BARRY D. CAPONI

iUniverse, Inc.
Bloomington

Contrary to Popular Belief—Cold Calling Does Work!
Volume I: Effectiveness, the Art of Appointment Making

Copyright © 2011 by Barry D. Caponi

All rights reserved. No part of this book may be used or reproduced by any means, graphic, electronic, or mechanical, including photocopying, recording, taping or by any information storage retrieval system without the written permission of the publisher except in the case of brief quotations embodied in critical articles and reviews.

Special bulk discounts are available to corporations, professional organizations, and other organizations. For information, please contact the author at bcaponi@caponipg.com or by phone at (817) 224-9900.

iUniverse books may be ordered through booksellers or by contacting:

iUniverse
1663 Liberty Drive
Bloomington, IN 47403
www.iuniverse.com
1-800-Authors (1-800-288-4677)

Because of the dynamic nature of the Internet, any web addresses or links contained in this book may have changed since publication and may no longer be valid. The views expressed in this work are solely those of the author and do not necessarily reflect the views of the publisher, and the publisher hereby disclaims any responsibility for them.

Any people depicted in stock imagery provided by Thinkstock are models, and such images are being used for illustrative purposes only.

Certain stock imagery © Thinkstock.

ISBN: 978-1-4620-0222-1 (sc)
ISBN: 978-1-4620-0224-5 (dj)
ISBN: 978-1-4620-0223-8 (ebook)

Printed in the United States of America

iUniverse rev. date: 05/01/2011

Contents

ACKNOWLEDGMENTS

Many of the books I've read over the years have started with the authors making what sounded—to me—like self-serving comments about how difficult they found writing their book. So now that I've completed my first book, I find that I'm no different—and only now can I truly empathize with them.

When my wife, Nancy, and I started our sales training and consulting business at the beginning of 2004, I found that I loved to write, so I've been blogging and writing articles right from the beginning. Piece of cake to compile that work into a book, right? Trust me; it is not as easy as one might think.

The reason I bring that up—other than perhaps also appealing for the *sympathy vote* myself—is that I have many people to thank for helping me on my odyssey.

First of all, I must thank my sister, Deb Newman, for being the first to suggest that I write a book. She has been after me for a long time and has never given up on me—although she must have thought about using a very large stick from time to time to get me to do it!

I also must thank my wife, who put up with the very early mornings, late nights, and long weekends away from her and the things we like to do together (even when on vacation) that it took to get it done.

Thank you to my good friend, Bob Howard, founder and president of Contact Science, LLC, whose brainchild, Klpz, is the science of the Art & Science of Appointment Making. So many times he helped me take my thoughts and put them to paper in a more concise manner.

Thanks to my colleagues and good friends Stu Schlackman and Steve Bregman, who took the time to read this book and gave me solid feedback—as well as one of my best friends, author Richard Merrick, who also invested a lot of his time to do the same.

Lastly, thanks to my brother Todd, who actually was the one that got me into this business that I love. Thanks to you all.

FOREWORD

Sales are the life of every company. Without sales, we don't exist—period. Every company's number-one concern when it comes to selling is what's in the pipeline this month, this quarter, this year, and how will we improve our position to make our budget.

There are many excellent books in the market today that tell us how to interface with the prospect or with our existing customers. They focus on strategic selling, questioning techniques, presentation skills, and how to close the deal. The problem is that there is not much out there that addresses the most important and toughest job in sales: getting new face-to-face appointments with new prospects. There is a huge difference between pipeline management and pipeline building. Selling truly starts with appointment-setting, and that's where successful sales professionals invest the right amount of time and effort to ensure success in improving the size of their pipeline.

Barry Caponi is the expert in the sales industry when it comes to appointment-setting. He has been training world-class sales organizations for the past decade to better understand the art and science of appointment-setting. Barry's approach is the authoritative source when it comes to improving the effectiveness and the efficiency of the challenge, and this book is a great reference manual for his methods. Even though there are many great lead-generation programs today and excellent tools for referral marketing and networking via social media, sales organizations still need to make calls to set appointments. Barry has developed a methodology that will get anyone more appointments.

As a sales trainer who has written two books on selling and has spent twenty-five years in the selling arena, I can assure you that this book addresses the entire set of tools, processes, and skills that are needed to be successful when it comes to a salesperson's biggest fear: *the cold call.*

Whether we are seasoned sales professionals or just starting out, this book is a must-read for any of us who are interested in building a robust pipeline that leads to success in selling year after year. Barry knows the challenges sales professionals face and his ColdCalling101™ *formula* is one that works—regardless of whether calling warm leads or cold names. I use it for my own business. Enjoy his approach as he addresses this facet of selling in a very practical way!

Stu Schlackman,
President of Competitive Excellence and author of *Four People You Should Know* and *Don't Just Stand There, Sell Something.*

WHAT IS THIS BOOK ABOUT?

This book (and its companion, *Volume II: Efficiency, the Science of Appointment Making)* is about the business process of getting enough targets *into* the pipeline through the discipline of telephone prospecting (even if we begin the process by canvassing door to door).

Let's face it—very few of us like to cold call, and many of us actually claim that we don't do it at all. In reality, however, most of us go through the process of asking strangers for appointments every day. We just don't call it cold calling. To illustrate that point, I've included a blog in this book that addresses this in detail. It's entitled, *There's actually no difference between a cold call and a warm call.*

This set of two books is about three things: defining the business process of appointment-setting, explaining why the process is necessary for almost all sales professionals, and showing how to do it more *effectively* and *efficiently*.

A word is probably in order here about the slightly different subtitles of these two books. In the first volume, I focus on telephone prospecting effectiveness—i.e., doing the right things. In the second volume, the emphasis is on telephone prospecting efficiency: improving your prospecting ratios so that you get the highest possible return from your efforts.

THE IMPORTANCE OF THE DISCIPLINE.

Two salesmen who haven't seen each other in weeks meet in a coffee shop for lunch.

"How's your day?" asks the first salesman.

"Great! I'm following up on several good leads. I've got a great prospect I'm working with—and I'm waiting on a PO from another client."

"Yeah," says the other salesman, "I haven't sold anything today either."[1]

There are three morals to this story.

1. Conversations like this emanate from an empty pipeline.

2. A continuing flow of closed sales comes from a full pipeline—and a full pipeline comes from a continuous flow of Initial Appointments.

3. "Make no mistake," I said in *Is Cold Calling Really Dead? Searching for the Elusive Silver Bullet*, "at the end of the

day, whether the call is cold or warm, it almost always falls to one of us sales professionals to pick up the phone and dial the number that starts the dialogue that begins the buying process."

What this somewhat humorously attempts to point out is that the ability to set the Initial Appointment that begins the selling process is a critical process to all of us in sales. What it doesn't point out is that it is typically a neglected process. We like to say that it is the elephant in the sales bullpen. Everyone knows it's there, but because no one knows how to solve it, we just gingerly step around it.

Case in point, there are several books and websites out there today devoted to the concept that cold calling doesn't even work—or that it has become an obsolete or unnecessary discipline. (You can find some of them in the Other Resources section.)

If you read through the literature from those who say cold calling is obsolete or dead, you'll find a common theme: replace cold calling with pull marketing programs designed around technology and other activities to eliminate the need for it. Ideas such as website optimization, staying in contact through newsletters, e-mail, networking, and asking for more referrals from our existing customers are good ones, and they all work. As a matter of fact, we do them all and suggest that we all do as many as make sense in our own organizations to cut down on the number of cold calls that our teams must make. But here is the reality: if these pull programs don't generate enough Initial Appointments to fill the pipeline, we must still cold call. And, for the majority of us, they don't and we must.

For most of us in sales, the selling process begins with what we like to call an Initial Appointment. Initial Appointments may be face-to-face, over the phone, or through a web-based technology, but somehow or another, we've got to convince people (we call them targets) that it is in their best interest to open their calendar and make some time for that first meeting with us.

Here's what you need to know about this process. There are basically three sources for an Initial Appointment with a target. They are:

1. Lead-generation marketing campaigns that are designed to get people to raise their hand and tell us they are interested (this includes traditional advertising such as print, TV, radio, and direct mail, plus newer approaches such as social media);
2. Networking and referrals; and
3. Cold calling

But here's the rub with lead generation and referrals: just because someone expresses interest in our solution through one of our marketing programs doesn't mean that we'll get the appointment every time we call for one. Even strong referrals tell us no in exactly the same manner that cold call recipients do—they're just nicer about it because they don't want to offend the person who referred them to us. In other words, *the process we follow when asking for an Initial Appointment is exactly the same—regardless of whether the call is warm or cold.*

Therefore, the *skills, tools, and processes* we need to call marketing leads, to follow-up on referrals and networking connections are *exactly the same* as the ones we need to cold call. That also means that almost everyone who is charged to find new customers—or even expand his or her presence within existing customer accounts—must be able to *efficiently* and *effectively* set appointments.

WHO IS THIS BOOK WRITTEN FOR?

I've written this book from the sales manager's perspective. But what if you're not a sales manager? What if you're a small business owner, independent sales professional, or sales professional reporting to a sales manager? This book is also for you, because—like it or not—God has given us all the ultimate equalizer or a level playing field, if you will. It's defined by the same number of hours in each and every day. Those of us who are more *effective* and *efficient*, win. Those of us who are not, lose. It's as simple as that. And need I remind anyone that there are no monetary awards for second place in sales.

So regardless of whether you have responsibility for managing a team or just yourself, this book will have something in it to help you and/or your team become more *effective* and *efficient* at the business process of filling the pipeline.

WHO IS BARRY CAPONI AND WHY SHOULD I LISTEN TO HIM?

I have been selling my entire professional career. I've sold computer hardware and software solutions, property management services, life and health insurance, and of course the speaking engagements, sales consulting, and the training services I now sell.

All of these require mastering the business process of prospecting and appointment-setting. So not only have I been studying this process since starting my company in 2004, but I've had to set appointments to get those buying cycles going throughout my entire selling career.

I've been a sales manager at every level—from a front-line district sales manager to chief sales officer of a global company. I've had to manage sales professionals who also had to set appointments to get those buying cycles going. In those jobs, my main concern each day was about the insufficient and poorly qualified pipelines that I was being presented with and how to consistently fill them.

I've also personally sold solutions that required me to call at just about every level of management; as the price tags on what I was selling ranged from just a few thousand dollars to millions of dollars.

Of course, when selling life and health products, I also called upon individual consumers in addition to businesses.

I hope that this helps you answer, "Who is Barry Caponi?" However, what about, "Why should I listen to him?" Since founding the Caponi Performance Group, Inc., I've concentrated our focus on this business process of helping our customers consistently get more targets *into* the pipeline. But why did I choose to concentrate on that instead of the more traditional sales training curriculum of helping get prospects *through* the pipeline?

That one is an easy question to answer since I had no desire to make our job any more difficult than it had to be. Sales managers have consistently told us that, once in front of a target, their teams were pretty good at scoring runs—to borrow a baseball analogy. (This has not always been true, but that's a story for another day.) There are also many excellent methodologies and sales consultants available today to help in this more traditional segment of the selling process.

I decided to concentrate our efforts where our targets believe their biggest barrier to success has always been—getting enough "at bats." Therefore, since we already had one of the very best methodologies for improving the *effectiveness* of setting appointments, (*The Appointment Making Formula*™ or as we affectionately call it, *The Formula*), and had also found the best and most unique tool[2] in the market to improve the *efficiency* of the process, why not concentrate our efforts where there was the most perceived pain? Therefore, our brand—ColdCalling101™—was born.

Since there are a lot of very good methodologies out there to help us take prospects *through* the pipeline phase of selling, the key question we asked ourselves when first addressing this challenge was why it continues to be so difficult for sales teams to get targets *into* the pipeline.

Our research and experience with our customers led us to conclude that the answer to that question was that everyone has been operating under a basic and *mistaken assumption*—to get quality targets *into* the pipeline, we can just use the *same skills, tools, and processes* that work so well to move a prospect *through* the pipeline. After all, selling is selling, right? (See blog entitled *The skills that are necessary in the pipeline phase of selling are not the same as those required in appointment-setting.* As for the issues involved in the *efficiency* side of the process, they are addressed in Volume II.)

The result of this mistaken assumption—the application of the traditional pipeline-selling approaches to the challenge of setting appointments—has proven to be both *ineffective* and *inefficient.* For instance, many companies tried to address *efficiency* by using the same CRM, contact managers, and sales force management applications that they use to help them drive prospects through the pipeline. Other companies tried to address just their *effectiveness* challenges by applying the same scripting and objection-handling approaches they use in the pipeline. When neither approach succeeded in consistently feeding the pipeline, most sales managers fell back on the traditional mantra: "Make more dials!"

In reality, the primary goal is relatively simple—to achieve the required number of Initial Appointments with as few dials as possible in as short a time as possible. Yet the accomplishment of this goal is obviously not so simple.

So here's why you should listen to us. We've studied this portion of the selling process extensively and:

1. To our knowledge, our ColdCalling101™ solution is the only all-encompassing approach to meeting the appointment-setting challenge (e.g., we supply all the *skills, tools, and processes* of appointment-setting);

2. The tool (Klpz) we recommend was specifically designed to address the different challenges of the appointment-setting process;

3. The skills (*The Formula*) are also designed just for the appointment-setting process;

4. We provide tools for the sales manager that they've never had before—and we teach them how to use those to be a more effective coach and manager; and lastly

5. The use of our solution will *sustain the gains* over a long period of time.

Adopting the ColdCalling101™ approach has transformed many a sales team's whole approach to prospecting. As a matter of fact, those that do implement our methodology routinely double or better the number of Initial Appointments that their sales team was setting prior to using our comprehensive approach.

Additionally, as this book is written from the manager's point of view, let me take a moment and expand on the one element on this list that applies to us as managers since it is critical to the success of any implementation of our solution and it is what makes the inevitable gains sustainable.

We have provided managers with a more powerful set of tools and reports than we've ever had before. This is accomplished through the *science* (a tool called Klpz from a company called Contact Science) that allows us to see the entire process in all of its component parts, and provides the tools and processes for managers to easily *monitor, measure, and manage* it through quantitative metrics.

The first challenge for managers in the appointment-setting process has always been the lack of credible, accurate, or timely information. For example, many of us ask our sales professionals for the number of Initial Appointments that they set each week. Or perhaps we additionally ask for the number of dials that they make to set those appointments. How many of us believe what's in those reports? In our experience, the answer is a very few of us.

The disbelief in those numbers is not based entirely on what we might think, though. Sure, some of our lesser-performing charges fudge (I'm trying to be politically correct here) those reports, hoping to buy time to catch up. But there is also the undeniable truth that it is difficult to keep up with the data that goes into those reports. Anyone who has tried to keep track of the number of dials, conversations, voice mails left and returned, plus appointments set each day can attest to that. We get interrupted, people return calls when we're out of the office, we make calls from the road, we go from call to call with no time to record the results of the last call, etc. There are many reasons why those reports are inaccurate at best.

However, since we must make management decisions based on something, we make do with the information we've got. Those that are familiar with the old expression, "Garbage in, garbage out," know the dangers of doing so. So the major topic we'll cover in Volume II is how to improve our underlying data—and how to turn it into manageable information.

A final note: this segment of the sales process is constantly evolving. For instance, technology (voice mail and e-mail in particular) has changed the landscape of appointment-setting over the past five years. And, while the approach we teach will work today, we encourage you to always be fine-tuning as your landscape changes. To help with that, I encourage you to sign up to follow our Tweets (announcing the topic of that week's blog) on Twitter (www.Twitter.com/ColdCalling101), visit www.ColdCalling101.com/blog, and watch for us on www.YouTube.com/ColdCalling101 to keep up with more on the skills, tools, and processes necessary to be successful at appointment-setting as they continue to evolve.

HOW DID THIS BOOK COME TO BE?

As you might imagine, many of my customers have been clamoring for me to publish a book for quite some time. They tell me that the workbooks their teams are provided during our Prospector's Academies™, although great learning tools during the academy, just don't have enough of the detail of what we covered to act as stand-alone reference tools somewhere down the road.

I've also had a number of colleagues who provide sales consulting in the pipeline phase of the selling process encourage me to do so as they also see the logic in our approach (not to mention the results in some of our joint customers).

All of that got me to begin writing a blog on this topic (www.coldcalling101.com/blog) back in July 2007. I generally publish one a week, so I've written quite a few over the years.

Lastly, it has come from two points of frustration with some of those others trying to provide competitive solutions to what we offer—or worse, an alternative panacea to the challenge. We've already agreed that very few of us like to cold call. So why would anyone want to make this process any more difficult than it inherently is? Yet, at best, that is exactly what many of these solutions do—using those ineffective techniques just makes the task more difficult and frustrating. At worst, those that say cold calling (and therefore also by association, the need for appointment-making skills) is dead are misleading sales professionals to believe that they do not need to master this process at all—and that is an immense disservice. Sadly, not one of them has replaced the need for sales professionals to know how to pick up the phone and be both *effective* and *efficient* at the process that begins the selling process. As a matter of fact, this bad advice has probably cost some good sales professionals their jobs over the years.

Here's the latest example of the latter category: the advent of social media. I can't tell you how many sales managers and sales professionals told me in 2009, when sites such as LinkedIn, Facebook, and Twitter became mainstream, that they didn't need our services anymore because they were going to be using social media to get those Initial Appointments. The reality is that social media, at worst, is a time-waster and at best is just another warm lead generator where good appointment-setting techniques are still needed to convert them into appointments.

At the end of the day, we sales professionals are the ones who are *ultimately held responsible* for getting in front of enough targets to make our number. And, regardless of the target being warm or cold, we need to master the skills that are specific to the business process of using the telephone to set an Initial Appointment.

At last count, I had nineteen different books on cold calling and appointment-setting sitting on my bookshelf, so I eat, drink, and sleep this stuff. Of those nineteen books, there are only three (see Other Resources at the back of the book) whose methodologies and techniques I agree with in some form or fashion. In other words, most of the stuff that's out there doesn't work in the long run. The reason that they seem to in the short run is that almost any process will work when we do find those few targets that are *in the market* when we call them. Also, any consistently applied process is better than just *winging it* as most sales professionals have been doing for years and still do today.

The ones I disagree with are all based on the same foundation. They spend an inordinate amount of time trying to perfect the ideal opening *pitch* that will immediately *wow* the target into believing that they just have to meet with us. Then when the target still says, "No," they attempt to overcome the no with logic. At this point, logic has not yet entered the target's mind.

Since most of our targets don't believe that they are *in the market* for what we're selling when we call them, those logical approaches do not work as well as we think they should. Most of the negative responses have little to do with reality or logic since they are nothing but what we call *conditioned knee-jerk responses* designed to get us off the phone. Therefore, logic doesn't work very well until we can get them past that first panic reaction of, "Oh shoot," (fill in your own word there if you don't like *shoot*), "another sales professional! How am I going to get rid of this one?" (See blog entitled *Top ten biggest mistakes cold callers make on the phone* for more on how and why our approach works so well.)

CONCLUSION

I don't expect this book—even combined with Volume II—to answer *all* of your questions. But I do believe that it will give you hope that there is an overall answer out there to the challenge in general and will answer most of the most common questions we hear. As a matter of fact, I'd love to hear about your successes as you apply the answers you do find here.

There are two more resources that you have access to if you are of the *do-it-yourself* ilk. I have written two white papers that are available on my website at www.caponipg.com. One is a senior management paper that describes the challenges of the entire process and describes what the alternatives are. It is called: *Is Cold Calling Really Dead? Searching for the Elusive Silver Bullet.* The second is more of a how-to white paper that describes how to actually write the scripts for the opening and explains how we handle the, "no," we invariably hear. It is called: *The Appointment Making Formula™: The Secret to Setting More Appointments.*

Both, by the way, are free. However, if you're like most of our customers and don't have the time it takes to implement a comprehensive program yourself, I'd be remiss if I didn't offer our assistance to help your team double or better the number of Initial Appointments that they are setting presently just as our customers do every day.

If you'd like to figure out exactly what that would do to your bottom line, check out the Sales Activity and ROI Calculator page on our website. You can also find a description of what we do and how we do it there as well.

But regardless of how you proceed, I wish you success in all your endeavors and thank you for the opportunity to earn your business.

To your prospecting success,

Barry D. Caponi

HOW TO USE THIS BOOK
AS A REFERENCE MANUAL

The purpose of publishing these chosen blogs is to allow you to quickly find and read a tip on a topic that may be of current concern. The alternative was to force you into reading an entire book on a methodology in order to find that useful nugget of information to solve that particular concern. In other words, it was designed to be used as a *reference manual*.

For instance, let's say that you've invested the time, energy, and money to create a set of Best Practices, including an opening script and how to counter the "no" that they seem to always hear, but you can't get the team to learn and use them. They tell you that they don't want to sound *canned* or like the proverbial telemarketer reading a script, so they continue to wing it, much to your consternation.

Here's what you would do. Go to the Contents pages and look through the blog titles. Depending on the way your charges are stating their reluctance to internalizing what you've created for them, you might find the following entries of interest in determining how to solve this dilemma.

* *The need for personal improvement.*

- *The skills that are necessary in the pipeline phase of selling are not the same as those required in appointment-setting.*
- *There's actually no difference between a cold call and a warm call.*
- *Practice makes perfect. The need to internalize scripts.*
- *The tone of our voice is more important than the content of our message.*
- *The impact of voice inflection on effective appointment-setting.*
- *The value of using scripts.*
- *Cold calling, the whac-a-mole, and the teleprompter.*

CHAPTER 1:
GENERAL TOPICS

General topics include subjects that are important to understanding the challenge of appointment-setting in general, but not quite pure art or science.

For instance, we cover the importance of appointment-setting, whether it is really necessary, the top ten mistakes that sales professionals make when attempting to set appointments, why the skills, tools, and processes that work in pipeline selling don't work in appointment-setting, etc.

It is a good primer to understanding how we view the challenge of appointment-setting. It is also a great primer to help you understand why your teams struggle at this step in the selling process.

THE NEED FOR PERSONAL IMPROVEMENT.

Sharpening the saw. Are you a member of the 4-4-4 Club for this year yet?

In *The 7 Habits of Highly Effective People,* Stephen Covey addresses renewal and self-improvement in the last chapter. He calls it *sharpening the saw.*

The term 4-4-4 Club is not Covey's, but it still hits the mark. Each of the three numbers relates to setting annual goals for sharpening the saw.

- Read 4 books each year
- Listen to 4 CDs each year
- Attend 4 seminars each year

Lastly, we should be investing 3 percent of our annual income back into ourselves.

Congratulations on making the effort to read this book. Did you know that less than 10 percent of all sales professionals will do anything this year to improve themselves? How are you and your team stacking up on the remaining suggestions?

We hope that our websites—www.coldcalling101.com, www.caponipg.com, and www.contactscience.com—will help fulfill your requirements in the area of sales improvement! As I mentioned in the Introduction, sign up to follow me on Twitter/ColdCalling101 to be notified about each week's blog topic. It will help you quickly determine whether the topic is something that is of interest to you.

IS COLD CALLING REALLY NECESSARY?

Very few of us like to cold call, so how do we figure out whether we need to cold call at all?

It's really a pretty simple process as there are basically only three sources for an Initial Appointment with a target. They are:

1. Lead-generation marketing campaigns that get people to raise their hands and tell us they are interested

2. Networking and referrals

3. Cold calling

To figure out whether we need to cold call (and how much if we do), follow this formula:

1. How many Initial Appointments do I need in a year to hit my sales goal? (You can use our Sales Activity and ROI Calculator that you can find on our website www.caponipg.com or send me an e-mail at book@caponipg.com.)

2. From that number, subtract the following:
   a. The number of Initial Appointments we get from marketing programs
   b. The number of Initial Appointments we get from networking activities and referrals from customers

3. Whatever gap there is between the number we computed in Step 2, subtracted from the result in Step 1, is the number you'll need to fill with cold calling. There is no other alternative.

Two last caveats:

1. Cold calling works best when we do it on a consistent basis, so we must figure out how many we need on average and do some *every* day—or at least weekly

2. Marketing, networking, and referrals can sometimes not generate what we expected—or an economic downturn can cause us to need more. Make sure you're looking at your results each week to see whether you need to open the cold calling spigot to make up the difference. Did I mention that there is no other alternative?

THE NECESSARY SKILLS IN THE PIPELINE PHASE OF SELLING ARE NOT THE SAME AS THOSE REQUIRED IN APPOINTMENT-SETTING

There are four key differences.

Many sales managers that we talk to operate under the assumption that because their sales team—once in front of a target—can move that target through the pipeline effectively, they are also properly equipped and capable of getting a target *into* the pipeline. After all, selling is selling, isn't it? The sale—or objective—is just different in the case of trying to set an Initial Appointment, right?

Unfortunately, the answer is no. And this misunderstanding of the differences has created what we like to call the e*lephant in the sales bullpen.* It is apparent to everyone that enough Initial Appointments are not being set, but the root cause is not pursued. Instead, sales managers ignore the elephant and utter the old mantra, "Make more dials!"

This four-part blog explores the four major differences: the Beginning Repartee, the Pace of the Exchange, the Types of Responses heard from the target, and Preparation to Succeed.

1. *Beginning Repartee.* If our target has agreed to an appointment with us, the opening moments of the call, although perhaps not yet openly friendly, are at least collegial or warm. That happens because our target has already determined to invest time with us so they are open to the conversation and to us.

   On a cold appointment-making call, the opposite is true. They have not yet agreed that there is value in even talking—let alone meeting with us (even on a referral call). The reasons for that are twofold. The first is that they don't think that they need what we're selling yet, so why would they *need* to have this conversation? The second reason is that we're interrupting them from doing something—so they don't even *want* to talk with us. The result is that they'll do anything, including *lie* to us, to get us off the phone. Hence, the term *cold call* as the target's behavior towards us is cold. What that means is that the call begins as being *adversarial*.

On the Initial Appointment, the normal conversational skills that we all have developed throughout our life are at play. Not so on the cold call. The skills necessary to counter that initial negative response and get the targets to open their minds for a moment to a conversation about how our value proposition has helped others—and hence potentially them—are not needed or practiced in the pipeline half of the selling process.

2. *Pace of the Exchange.* When in front of a target in a sales call, the pace of the conversation is generally deliberate, calculated, and measured. When the target asks us a question, we can take a moment to think about the question before answering. It is totally acceptable to do so. As a matter of fact, it can be misconstrued as a sign of disrespect if we don't ever seem to take a moment to think about what is asked and always seem to be quick with what could be taken as a *canned* response.

On an appointment-setting call, the pace is accelerated. Our targets generally answer very quickly by falling back on their favorite *Conditioned Knee-Jerk Response* (i.e., their typical way of getting sales professionals off the phone quickly). They don't need to think about it—it is a reflex.

We must respond just as quickly—or we risk being hung up on or being put on the defensive. The whole conversation is conducted at the speed of a Nolan Ryan fastball. So if we're not practiced at handling the few standard negative responses that we hear consistently, we'll not have near the results that we'd like or need.

3. *Types of Responses.* Because a target has agreed to meet with us, he or she is willing to hear our story and share his or her own to help determine whether it makes sense to move forward with us. This means that the target's responses to our questions are more apt to be based on logic.

   On a cold call, the responses we generally hear are more of a knee-jerk response designed to get us off the phone. Many times, those responses are not even true, although they may contain a grain of truth. If you'll think about it, each of us has our own favorite we use when cold called.

   Applying logic to targets' lies does no good because there is no logic in their response. Therefore, when we call people, we must give them a vehicle to retreat from that opening knee-jerk response in such a way that they save face and open their mind to a short conversation regarding what we've done for others to address a challenge or supply a benefit.

   We must *counter* their negative response, using a transition that provides them the ability to save face (a lot of our customers felt the same way) and then ask a question that will open their mind to a short conversation by asking one of our *Bridge Questions*™³. (By the way, our counter technique works just as well when the target actually gives us a true response.)

4. *Preparation to Succeed.* When in front of a target during the pipeline phase of the selling process, our preparation for the meeting should definitely include some planning. However, we cannot plan for all contingencies. That means that much of our success is based on our ability to

think on our feet since each situation is at least slightly different.

On a cold call, there are only a few responses that we'll hear if we deliver the same message each time we approach someone. To accomplish that, we must internalize or memorize our opening approach to limit the responses we'll hear and also internalize or memorize the responses we'll use to counter those. We'll also need to practice them so that they roll off the tongue like normal conversation.

TOP TEN BIGGEST MISTAKES COLD CALLERS MAKE ON THE PHONE

1. Believe the first negative response that we hear.

There are only two ground rules our targets play by when they receive a cold call and we ignore them at our peril.

When we place a cold call, we must understand that the person we're calling really doesn't think they *need* to talk to us. As a matter of fact, our surveys show that less than 5 percent of targets in any sales professional's universe of potential customers *believe that they are in the market* for what we're selling when we call them.

We must also understand that we are interrupting our target from doing something when we call, so they don't *want* to talk to us.

The result of those two rules is that they will do anything, *including lie to us*, to get us off the phone. Most cold calling methodologies teach us to counter their statement using a logical argument (or power benefit) to convince them that they should meet with us. But if they're lying to us, why would we think logic would work against a statement that is not true?

I don't know about you, but I don't have enough time to make calls until I find that 1–5 percent that is currently *in the market*. Since half of them seem to be too busy right then anyway, we must employ a different approach to get them past this *knee-jerk* reaction (we call them negative responses or conditioned responses) designed to get us off the phone before we can apply any kind of logic to their response.

The most powerful technique of *The Formula* is called the *Bridge Question*[4]. This concept is what differentiates us from all other appointment-setting methods. It is used to accomplish any one or more of the following objectives:

- Most typically, it provides us the ability to *bridge* from the target's conditioned knee-jerk response (negative response) into an open minded, albeit short, conversation to share what we've done for others (our value proposition);

- Provides us the ability to expand on our value proposition, which will help reduce no-shows and cancellations;

- Should they ask us a question (which we must answer), it *bridges* us back into control of the conversation; and

- Qualify if desired.

Here then, are the rules (or tests) for the application of *Bridge Questions*. Each question has a specific purpose:

- It should get us an answer to help qualify the target and get them into a *short* conversation to build value for the meeting;

- It must call for a relatively short answer;

- We must be able to predict and control the answer with, "That's exactly why we need to get together. How *is* Tuesday at 2:00?"; and

- Generally, open-ended questions that qualify as *how*, *what*, or *why* questions work best.

Here's an example of one of the best I've seen:

"How many months of home care could your current financial portfolio absorb before it would begin to affect your retirement plans?" This *Bridge Question* is used by one of our long-time customers, Newman Long Term Care, out of Minneapolis, Minnesota (one of America's leading experts on long term care insurance, by the way). They use it to counter the "I don't need it," negative response that they hear more often than any other. The typical answer is, "I don't know," which is why it is so successful—the sales professional can then respond with passion and belief, the response shown in point number 3, above.

2. Tell the target all about what we can do for them.

Remember that they don't think they need what we're selling, so why do we think this approach will work? Instead, we should tell them about the results someone else got from using what we sell. (All of us—okay, maybe just most of us—think that everyone else knows some little secret that we don't that's made them more successful than we are.)

There are three steps to defining the message and then a very simple *formula* to apply it.

- Write out the best success stories of someone using our solutions we can think of. Include these five components:
    a. What were the challenges facing our customer?
    b. How did we address those challenges?
    c. What were the results?
    d. What did the customer tell us were the benefits of those results?
    e. Can we use any of the names attached to these stories?

- Again, using those same success stories as a reference point, list:
    a. What were the features each of those current customers purchased; and
    b. What were the benefits those customers derived from those features?
- Combine our answers and rank them in the order that we believe customers buy from us.
- Apply it as follows:

  "The reason I was specifically calling you today was that our customers have had a lot of success *(insert most powerful approach above)* and I'd like to stop by your office and share with you how they were able to accomplish that."

  If you'd like to read a more robust article about how to write powerful cold call value propositions, go to our website at www.caponipg.com, find the articles archive and look for the article entitled *Three Simple Steps to Create a Powerful Cold Calling Value Proposition*.

3. Assume that we can help them do what they are currently doing—better than they are currently doing it.

"I can save you money over what you're paying today!" "I can make you more productive and save you time!" Ever had someone call you with a message like these? If it's not in the opening message, a lot of cold callers resort to this approach as we try to talk the person we're calling into meeting with us. When I hear that, I get even more upset at the interruption than I was when I realized that it was a cold call.

We lose credibility when we make those types of statements because it assumes that we have intimate knowledge of their current situation—and in most cases we don't. (This does assume we haven't done our homework and do know that we can help them. If we did though, the message would still be slightly different—but that's a topic for another day.)

How do we know what they're paying or how well they're doing? For that matter, how do we even know they use what we're selling? We *do* want to find out if we can help them, but let's not use the assumptive position that we can. It's insulting and makes us sound like the proverbial telemarketer.

One last thought. Go ahead and use this approach if you've been able to help 100 percent of the prospects you entered into a buying cycle with—because you're selling the proverbial better mousetrap. Take advantage of it while you can. It won't last long.

4. Not internalizing our message.

One of the biggest reasons I hear sales professionals use when they say they don't want to cold call is that they don't want to sound like the proverbial telemarketer. They complain that those callers just seem to be reading their scripts in a monotone voice.

Actually, I couldn't agree more. That occurs when we don't take ownership of our message and internalize it until we sound conversational. If we're reading a script, we *do* sound like the proverbial telemarketer.

Only 7 percent of effective communications is derived through the words we use. The biggest percentage of effective communications on a phone call comes from tonality (38 percent). Therefore we must not only *own* our message, we must deliver it with passion. There is only one way that the passion can come through—and that's if we know what we're going to say so we can concentrate on how we deliver it.

You do believe in what you sell, don't you? Well then, know what you're going to say and deliver it with passion.

5. Winging it on each call.

Above, we talked about how not to sound like we're reading our script by internalizing our message. The other alternative is to wing it on each call so that our message is different each time.

The problem with *winging it* is that if we deliver a different message each time, we can't predict and control the responses we'll get. That makes the task of handling those negative responses even more difficult.

Remember, that if we deliver the same message each time, we'll get the same few negative responses each time. Getting the same negative responses each time reduces the number of counters that we've got to learn and practice.

Don't fall into the trap of thinking that winging it is the easy way out. It's not. It's one of the things that make cold calling feel so difficult.

6. Asking leading questions.

This is an example of one of my favorites I hear from time to time, "You would like to save money wouldn't you?" Remember that less than 5 percent of the people we call think that they are in the market for what we're selling when we call. If they don't think they need us and don't want to talk to us, this kind of question just backs them into a corner. (How can they answer no to that question without sounding like an idiot?) It is offensive, and does nothing but tick them off even more at the interruption, making the call even more confrontational.

7. Not leaving voice mails—or leaving long-winded ones.

The advertising industry says that it takes seven to nine touches for someone to even remember our name, let alone our value proposition, so why waste the effort involved in making the call and not leave a message?

Think of it as personal advertising. So what if they don't return this particular call? They don't always call when they see one of our ads, do they? And what better way to leave a message that should mean something to this particular target? It's better than advertising!

If that's not enough of a reason for you, think about this. When we make a call to someone, most of the time investment has already been spent. You've had to review your list of targets to call, determine who will be called, determine where you are in the process with this particular target, dial the phone, get through the phone tree, etc. Our benchmarks indicate that, at this point, we've already invested a minimum of four or five minutes without the right automation, and 1.5 to 2.5 minutes with the right automation (see below). So what's another ten to fifteen seconds? (Your messages shouldn't be any longer than that anyway.)

In order to craft well thought out, concise voice mails, go back to how to create our best value propositions as laid out in Rule No. 2 and use those. Each time we call during a cycle, we recommend leaving a different message. And if you've got the automation to do it efficiently (we recommend a product called Klpz from Contact Science), send a coordinated e-mail to double the number of *touches* in each attempt.

8. When leaving voice mails, not saying our phone number s-l-o-w-l-y and repeating it.

As Andy Rooney might whine, "Have you ever gotten a voice mail with a telephone number left so fast that you had to listen to it multiple times before you got the whole number?" Well, I have and I know that you have because it is all too common.

You know what I do with those voice mails? If I can't get the number after the second attempt, I delete it. And, heck, I think every cold call to me is a prospect, so I've got an incentive to listen. Trust me—the rest of the world is not so kind.

In our Prospector's Academies on ***The Formula,*** we actually role-play leaving voice mails. What we hear a lot in those role-plays is nervousness. That nervousness generally represents itself in speed. Slow down a little bit. If you think that your voice mail is too long, then it is. Work on shortening it, but make sure you leave your number twice and say it s-l-o-w-l-y.

By the way, if you think that you needn't repeat it because you're leaving it from a landline to a landline, think about how often we retrieve our office voice mails with our cell phones? Ever had one of those clicks happen that seems to cover up a word or number? That causes us to have to listen to the whole message again, right? Make it easy on our targets to do business with us! Leave your number twice and say it s-l-o-w-l-y.

9. Not letting the target know when this will be the last.

Many participants in ***The Formula's*** Prospector's Academies say that no one returns voice mails anyway, so why bother leaving them? Well, here's the biggest reason of them all to do so!

Our methodology includes the practice of leaving voice mails—and we've talked about the many advantages of doing so in these blogs in the past, so I won't repeat them all here. But think about this for a moment.

We've invested (hopefully) a lot of time developing the value propositions that we want our targets to hear regarding why they should meet with us. Why? Because we know that there are people out there that *are* in the market for what we sell when we call. So we know that we'll hit targets that do want to talk with us from time to time, right?

One of the two ground rules of cold calling, though, is that we are interrupting people when we call them, which means we must acknowledge that they're busy doing something when we call—even if they happen to be in the market for our solution. If we do not inform them that this is the last time we will call for a while, they may not call us back assuming (incorrectly) that we'll try again later.

Disciples of *The Formula* consistently report back that they get more returned voice mails off of this move-on message than any other.

To implement this technique, the first thing we need to do is determine how many attempts we'll make to reach a target prior to moving on to another. (We call that a cycle.) When we get to the last call, try something like this:

"Good morning, Mark. My name is Barry Caponi, and I'm the president of the Caponi Performance Group. As you know, I've left you several messages over the past few weeks, and although I'm persistent, I certainly don't want to be a pest. If you've been as busy as most of my customers are, but meaning to return my call, please do so since I'm looking forward to talking with you. If you can't, I won't bother you again right now, but will call you back again in a few months if you don't mind. My number is (817) 224-9900—that's (817) 224-9900. Thanks and I look forward to hearing from you."

You'll be pleased with the result when implementing this technique!

10. Calling the same day and/or time of day over and over again, or calling the same person over and over again the same day.

Albert Einstein once said that the definition of insanity is "doing the same thing over and over, but expecting different results."

One of the basic tenets behind *The Formula* is having a plan (we call them Best Practices) and then employing technology (we use a specialized tool called Klpz that works as a front end to CRMs —www.contactscience.com) to track what you do so that we can better leverage what works and change what doesn't.

Every industry and target group has windows that are better

than others are for contacting them. The challenge is to figure out what works best for them and for us. I've heard sales professionals say that they make a hundred dials a day! Remember that the devil is in the detail.

Activity—or working hard—alone will not dictate success. It is not until we take a look at the individual elements of a calling plan (Best Practice) that we are able to begin to improve our performance. Are we only calling ten different people ten times per day? Are we always calling between eight and nine o'clock in the morning? Are we always calling on Monday?

In order to improve our performance, we must monitor what we do, measure what we do, and manage (or change) what we do.

If you call the same target multiple times per day and don't leave voice mails, you might also want to think about this for a second. In this world of caller ID, do you really think that your targets don't know you're a cold caller when your number shows up on their caller ID multiple times during the day? Remember that more and more people are using voice mail to screen.

What is the moral of this story? We need to think about what we do and why we do it. Then monitor the activity, measure the results, and manage accordingly.

THERE'S ACTUALLY NO DIFFERENCE BETWEEN A COLD CALL AND A WARM CALL.

Contrary to popular belief, there really is no difference between what happens on a cold call versus a warm call.

In our Prospector's Academies, we constantly hear, "I don't cold call. I network and follow-up on marketing-generated leads." So what is the difference between a *cold* call and a *warm* call?

There are four components to an appointment-making call regardless of whether it is cold or warm. The acronym is ARCA.

1. The **A**pproach

2. The target's **R**esponse (No)

3. Our **C**ounter

4. Asking for the **A**ppointment again

On a warm call, the Approach will vary slightly because we want to invoke either the name of the person who suggested that we call or the fact that they had asked us to contact them through a marketing program of some kind. The process and techniques we use to enlist the help of a gatekeeper, leave a message, send a coordinated e-mail, gain their attention, introduce ourselves, etc., is the same on any of these warm calls or a cold call.

If we really think about it, the target's response is also generally the same as on a cold call. They're just nicer about it. A referral target may say, "Hey, I appreciate Barry suggesting you call, but we're all set in that area." That's because in very few instances does the referrer know the target's business in enough detail to know they need us, can afford us, and that the timing is right for the call.

Even in the case of an inbound request for information from a lead-program, we sometimes are surprised by a negative response to a request for an appointment. However, it's not uncommon for an inbound request to be a tire-kicker or information-gatherer and not someone that's *in the market* right now for what we are selling. Maybe they just want us to *send something*. Certainly this does not happen all the time, but it happens more than we think.

There are also many times that a different challenge occurs on these calls—the temptation to *sell* on the appointment-making call because of their interest. So how do we keep from falling prey to this? Easy—we use the same process we do on a cold call to provide only enough value to get the appointment.

The reason that our curriculum is called *The Formula* even though we talk a lot about cold calling—is that the process or *formula* that we apply in a warm call also applies in a cold call. It's all appointment-setting—and we must be prepared in order to be successful.

THE VALUE OF KNOWING OUR METRICS

If we don't know how to effectively take someone who does not believe they are *in the market* for what we are selling when we pick up the phone and call, we will have to make many more calls for each appointment we set than we need or want to—and most of us have limited time to invest in cold calling.

Our surveys consistently show that less than 5 percent of any universe of targets *believes* that they are in the market for what we're selling when we call. If we take our target's word for it, less than five out of every hundred people we *talk to* should have an interest in meeting with us when we call. Our experience and calling metrics teach us that we'll not be able to convince all of those to meet with us for a variety of reasons, but let's assume for the sake of argument that we can.

Assumptions:
- Average time per dial = 6 minutes without Klpz, 3 minutes with it (includes prep time, calling, conversing, and recording the results)—trust me, we've documented it
- Typical Conversation Ratio = 10 percent (Dial to Conversations)
- Typical Appointment Ratio = 20 percent (Conversations to Appointments)
- Closing Ratio = 20 percent (Initial Meeting to Close)
- Percent *in the market* = 5 percent

Based on these averages, if we dial the phone a thousand times, we'll get through to fifty people. Of those fifty conversations, we'll only run into 2.5 that are in the market for what we're selling right now. Even assuming that they're all willing to meet with us, we've now invested six thousand minutes (one hundred hours) to get those appointments. So how much does our average sales professional make an hour? Is it worth it just to play the numbers game—or should we be learning how to convince some of those people that we've got something that others in their position have benefitted from? You do the math...

CHAPTER 2:
THE ART OF APPOINTMENT-MAKING

The Art is all about skills and effectiveness. It's why we win. It's what we say to get through to the person we wish to meet with, and then how well we do at converting those conversations into Initial Appointments.

Most appointment-making methodologies have us concentrate the majority of our effort on the opening message and then teach us to handle those first objections we receive with logical responses. The problem with that approach is that it doesn't work nearly as well as we think it should. That is because of two ground rules our targets instinctively play by:

1. Surveys show that less than 5 percent of our universe of targets believes that they are in the market for what we are selling when we call them--so they don't think they *need* to talk to us.

2. No matter when we call, we are interrupting that person from doing something—so they don't *want* to talk to us.

The result is that they'll do anything, include lie to us, to get us off the phone. Until we get them beyond the initial *knee jerk* reaction of saying anything (including lying to us) to get us off the phone, logic has no place in their thinking.

Our Art methodology, *The Formula,* acknowledges this reality of human nature and provides the *formula* to get our target to stop thinking about how to get us off the phone for a moment and open their minds to a short conversation where we *can* apply our value proposition through a proven, logical set of techniques to effectively counter their responses.

PRACTICE MAKES PERFECT. THE NEED INTERNALIZE SCRIPTS.

Practicing versus Doing—why do sports teams, who profess to play for *fun,* concentrate on practicing basic fundamentals skills (Art), and then specific plays (Best Practices) until they are second nature, yet we, who profess to belong to the *profession* of sales insist on winging it?

I was a sales manager at the district level up to the global level, and you know what, I never enforced (or recommended for that matter) having my teams practice any sales skills at weekly sales meetings. Attaining our revenue goals was *way* too important to take time out to practice the skills it takes to be efficient and effective. We would do it at a quarterly get together.

It was not until I became a sales consultant and trainer that I looked at skills improvement for what it is—getting better at what we do every day in order to sell more. A better fielding average or batting average *does* win more baseball games. It's why baseball teams record those statistics and practice those skills, not just in spring training, but pretty much before every game.

Every workshop I run, I hear the war stories of *big* sales lost because they were in at the wrong level, didn't ask the right questions, assumed something incorrectly, got there too late, etc. Why do I hear these stories? Because the proverbial light bulb comes on during our training and people realize that if they had only applied the skill we're talking about right then and there, they wouldn't have lost that deal. So what to do?

We should make a little time at each of our basic pipeline review meetings to practice (role-play) critical skills (fifteen minutes and make it fun). (Okay, maybe not at the last meeting before the end-of-the-quarter, but you get the idea.) Here's a list of appointment-making role-plays and exercises to use.

- For Gatekeepers and Decision Makers
    a. What are the most common challenges we face? List them, figure out how to handle them and then role-play them.
    b. What are the most common questions we hear on an appointment-making call? How will we answer them and then role-play them.
    c. What are the most common negative responses we hear? How will we handle them and then role-play them?
- What are the benefits our products or services bring to our customers? How do we build that into the reason we want to meet with someone? Role-play it.
- Ask your sales professionals to write down on a 3x5 card the answers to the following questions:
    a. What do we sell?
    b. What are the three biggest reasons our customers buy from us?
    c. What are the three biggest challenges we solve for our customers?
    d. How do our competitors answer those questions? (This is the biggie. It will help them realize why their targets respond the way they do. We're coming across as a "me too.") And if you

can't figure out how to adequately script your differences, call us.)

Particularly with the last exercise, don't be surprised if you get a bunch of different answers. Get marketing involved and standardize on a set of answers that work and get the team to internalize them.

COLD CALLING AND SCRIPTS. IT IS NOT NECESSARY TO MEMORIZE A SCRIPT.

How many times do we hear our sales professionals tell us they're much better on the phone when they don't memorize a script? Here's what we should be telling them in response...

What we really should be doing is internalizing it. Make it second nature so that it just rolls off the tongue. Let's hear yours."

When you ask what they say, be prepared for, "Well, I say something like this..." After they stumble through it, go back to the written scripts and ask them how that compares to what the company went through great lengths (not to mention expense) to develop. If they have a good reason for not liking the script, work with them to develop a new one. Then throw as many negative responses as you can at them and see how they handle them. Trust me; they'll stumble through that as well.

When sales professionals use the concepts in our methodology called *The Formula*, and then deliver the same message each time they call someone, one of the benefits they'll experience is a limited number of negative responses being heard. That will make their job easier.

So back to the original statement: It really isn't necessary to *memorize* the scrip, but they do need to *internalize* it.

What's the difference between memorization and internalization, you ask? Nothing really. But you can tell them that it means to take the script, put it in their own language (without changing the underlying message), and practice enough so that it rolls off the tongue just like conversation. Only then will they deliver the same message every time.

TARGETS PRIORITIZE THEIR DAYS, TOO.

Here's another reason to follow-up again.

In previous blogs we've talked about some metrics that should help us determine how many times we should attempt to contact a target. In this blog, we'll explore the more intangible reasons for that follow-up.

We all have more to do than we have time to do it. When we receive information that we find interesting, yet the topic is not yet a priority, what do *we* do with it? Most of us either have a stack for later review, or we just hope it will pop up again when we have more time.

How does this apply to cold calling and appointment-setting? Our targets have the same challenges. That means persistence wins because priorities change over time as does our availability to talk.

Have an ideal pursuit plan (we call it a Cycle) that includes the number of times we'll try and how often we'll try. Then follow it and don't give up.

WHEN IS ENOUGH, *ENOUGH* WHEN MAKING COLD CALLS?

Sales professionals many times ask me how many cold calling attempts to the same contact are too many.

This question actually comes in several flavors. For instance, how many times should I call this person today if I don't get through? How many times should I call this person over time until the law of diminishing returns kicks in and I'd be better off calling someone else for the first time rather than calling this same person again?

The reason this came to mind today is that I am in Chicago where

I gave a talk yesterday to the National Automated Merchandising Association. I'm staying with my dad who is retired. He went with me yesterday, so we were gone all day.

When we got home last night, he printed out a list of calls he had received during the day from his answering machine. There was one phone number on the list *fourteen* times. (I'm not kidding.) It was a stock broker who has never sold him anything, but has been calling him for a number of years. (Got to admire his persistence, I think.) When he spoke with the broker today (you guessed it, he called again), he tried to sell my dad a twenty year bond. My dad is 85 years old. Do the math—my dad did.

There are two points to this story. 1) This guy has talked to my dad on numerous occasions. He has never asked my dad what his investing goals are. He only knows my dad is a pretty active trader. So when he calls, most of the time he's trying to interest him in things that just don't make sense or that my dad has no interest in. 2) Why did this guy call my dad fourteen times and leave *no* messages? Did he think my dad wouldn't know he called that many times? Did he think that what he wanted to talk about couldn't stand on its own enough to get my dad to call him back? What kind of credibility does he have with my dad?

Moral of the story: It takes time to make a dial and time is money. We should invest those dials just like we would any other limited asset. Let's make sure it is worth it before we do it. Making another dial to the same number over and over again so that we kid ourselves into thinking we're busy is foolish. Calling someone and throwing mud at the wall to see if something sticks is also a waste of time. We should record our activity and look at the outcome. If we don't like the results, we should try something else. Don't keep doing the same thing expecting a different outcome. It's how Einstein defined insanity.

THEY MUST NOT BE INTERESTED BECAUSE THEY WON'T RETURN MY CALL.

Just because someone doesn't return our phone call or e-mail doesn't mean they can't or won't still become a future customer.

My Cycle for cold calls is 4x4x90. What that means is that I will make four attempts, every four days, and if I don't get through, I will Recycle them for ninety days and try again. I *always* leave a voice mail and on the fourth attempt, I will leave what I call a *move-on* message. In that voice mail, I will professionally convey the message that this will be my last attempt for a while, so if they have been meaning to call me back, now would be a good time. See *Top Ten Biggest Mistakes Cold Callers Make on the Phone*—No. 9—for an example. I get more calls returned from this message than all my other voice mails combined. As a matter of fact, it has been so successful that I have reduced my Cycle from five attempts to four. Why waste the time for the extra call?

Here's the lesson, though. When I ask people why they returned *this particular* message, the response is always the same. They tell me that they *did* want to speak with me, but that they *were* busy and figured sooner or later I'd get lucky and catch them. It was the sense of urgency that made them return the call.

The point is that just because they are not returning our calls, we cannot assume that they would not be a potential future customer. Don't give up on that name.

CALLER ID AND THE MYSTERY COLD CALLER.

So our sales professionals are thinking they're pulling a fast one on those that they are cold calling by calling with the caller ID on their phones blocked.

In one of our workshops the other day, one of our students proudly told us that they make their calls from a phone whose number shows up on the recipient's phone as *Caller ID Blocked*.

Let me ask a very simple question. When we receive a phone call and we look at our caller ID and it says *Blocked*, who do *we* think is calling?

Bottom line is that we're not doing ourselves any favors by hiding our identity from the person we're calling. Get them to unblock the block.

DOES E-MAIL WORK IN COLD CALLING CAMPAIGNS TO ACTUALLY SET APPOINTMENTS?

I was talking with a manager of one of our customers the other day and he told me he noticed on his team's Klpz reports that one of his sales professionals was making very few phone calls but was still hitting her activity goals of reaching out to targets each week. I asked him if she was setting as many appointments as she needed and he said no, her Initial Appointments had dropped substantially.

Without boring you with his travails, let me cut to the chase. I'm sure there are markets somewhere where e-mail trumps the phone for setting appointments, but I have yet to find it. If it's yours, I'd love to talk to you. In the meantime, here's what I think about e-mail in the appointment-making process.

My experience is that when sales professionals begin making more attempts to set appointments via e-mail than the phone, it's generally an indication of them avoiding making the calls and fooling themselves into thinking they're still working at it. My advice? Nip it in the bud *immediately* and get them back on the phone. (It's particularly seductive to do this in Klpz. That's because sending the already created e-mail that supports the voice mail requires only the same click of the mouse that is necessary to record the dial.)

Surveys show that less than 5 percent of our universe of targets is *in the marke*t for what we're selling when we contact them—and realistically I believe it's probably closer to 1 percent. Historically, good direct mail (and e-mail) campaigns show a 2 percent response rate, and that is *not* measured in appointments, but in interest only.

So what makes our intrepid sales professionals think they can better what marketing experts can do?

Only in a conversation can we convince the 99 percent that don't think they are *in the market* right now to see us by asking the right question based on their response. We can't do that in an e-mail.

So, use e-mail where it is effective, but use the phone when trying to set appointments.

WHEN AND HOW CAN E-MAIL SUPPORT COLD CALLING CAMPAIGNS?

E-mail is effective in a support role in the appointment-setting process.

E-mail is *good* for the following things:

- Increasing the number of *touch points* [1] in which the target sees and hears our key themes and messages;
- Long term territory building (this assumes we continue to pursue this target over time);
- Reinforcement of a verbal message;
- Finalizing (once a game of phone tag has begun regarding the time and place for an appointment), or to confirm an appointment;
- Delivering attachments that support the messaging;
- Delivering web links that support the messaging;
- Provide a way for a target to communicate back (even if they say no thanks); and
- A few of our targets actually prefer to communicate that way.

Bad uses for e-mail in appointment-setting:

---

1   The advertising industry rule of thumb is that it takes approximately seven to nine touches or touch points for a target to just recognize our name. So assuming we make eight dials per year (4 per Cycle x 2 Cycles) including a voice mail and an e-mail on each, we've touched this target sixteen times with multiple messages (assuming each attempt in a Cycle has a different advantage to our solution/message).

- Sending without a voice mail first as the only vehicle to deliver our message;
- When a conversation would be better (like when trying to set an appointment); and
- Closing a sale – appointment or purchase order

We believe that the biggest advantages e-mail can supply is being a quick and inexpensive, yet personal and reinforcing communication. So use it to support developing a warmer list to call for an appointment.

It should go without saying therefore that using e-mail as our primary vehicle for setting appointments is ineffective.

THE TONE OF OUR VOICE IS MORE IMPORTANT THAN THE CONTENT OF OUR MESSAGE.

Many times we run into sales professionals that are insistent on getting the content in message *perfect* before making any calls at all. We disagree.

UCLA did a study a number of years ago called the Law of Effective Communications. They found that there are three components to effective communications:

- 55% - non verbal
- 38% - tonality
- 7% - content

On a phone call, non-verbal communications (facial expressions, body language, etc.) is non-existent. The next most effective component is our tonality. Content is a very small component, although it's got to be there.

That means we need to have internalized our scripts so that we can concentrate on how we deliver the content. Be upbeat, professional, and passionate. If we believe in what we sell, we need to make sure that comes across in our voice.

We'll get appointments based on our belief if that comes through on the phone! Try it. You'll like the results!

THE IMPACT OF VOICE INFLECTION ON EFFECTIVE APPOINTMENT-SETTING.

In an earlier blog, I raised the issue of tone-of-voice when making an appointment-making call. Here are some related thoughts on the topic.

It takes more than a strong message to get someone to consider our request for an appointment when cold calling. Remember, our target's immediate and natural tendency will be to start thinking about how to get us off the phone as soon as they realize that we're selling something. That means they stop listening pretty quickly, so how do we increase the odds of getting them to hear what is important?

One way is through emphasizing the key points we want to make through the inflection we use in our voices. Here's a tip we teach in *The Formula* Prospector's Academies.

When we write our scripts down on a piece of paper, we *italicize* and **bold** the key points we want to emphasize when speaking them. Then as we start to memorize and practice them, we make sure our voices convey emphasis on those key points.

THE VALUE OF USING SCRIPTS.

Are you one of those sales people that *wing it* on every call? "I'm quick on my feet. I can handle anything!" you say. Well, there are three distinct reasons to use scripts in your appointment-making process.

In our appointment-making workshops I will always hear someone say they don't use scripts because they make them sound canned, much like the celebrated telemarketer. Here's what I say in response.

First and foremost, think back on the last *good* movie you saw. Do you think they *adlibbed* the whole movie? Of course not. They used a script, but they internalized it to sound like natural conversation. If we've not internalized our scripts, we're reading them, or worse, winging it. And if we're reading them, we *do* sound like the celebrated telemarketer.

So assuming we internalize what we're saying, here are three reasons why saying the same thing to open a conversation each time makes sense:

1. If we deliver the same message each time, we'll be able to predict the responses we'll hear (trust me, they will be the same);

2. If we can predict the responses we'll hear, we will be able to be prepared to handle them (shame on us if we've heard the same response a third time and we don't take the time to figure out how to handle it effectively); and

3. We will be a better listener if we're not worried about what we're going to say each time to those same responses. It is difficult at best to be listening to our target's response and simultaneously thinking about what we'll say next.

COLD CALLING, THE WHAC-A-MOLE AND THE TELEPROMPTER.

When do we need to memorize our scripts and when does reading the teleprompter suffice?

When we teach telephone prospecting, we sometimes get pushback from the participants regarding *memorizing* the opening scripts, transitions, counters, etc. that are part of their prepared Best Practices.

"That's a lot of work," we'll hear. The good news is that not everything needs to be memorized.

Where we need to have memorized things is basically in two areas. The first is the opening script. The second is how we'll counter the *few and predictable* negative responses we'll receive because *we did* memorize our opening script (which will limit the number of different types of negative responses we do get).

The opening must be memorized, but since it shouldn't be more than thirty or forty-five seconds anyway, it's not that difficult. Here's why:

1. We make our own job easier if we do. By delivering the same opening message *every* time, we can limit the responses we'll get into a manageable few. If we *wing it*, we open the door to all kinds of responses as there is a direct correlation between what *we* say and the responses we hear in return. So why would we want to make our job any more difficult?

2. We are better listeners if we're not worried about what *we're* going to say. We have all had the experience of someone we're talking with making a comment that is in direct conflict with something we've said. If it was a face-to-face sales call, we generally start thinking that this person isn't listening to us, right? At the very least it impacts the credibility they were trying to build. That happens when we're not listening with 100 percent of our attention.

The other area of our Best Practices we must internalize (memorize) is countering the negative responses we hear. Our ability to handle these quickly and effectively now becomes like the arcade game of *whac-a-mole*. When one pops up, we must respond as quickly as we can before it disappears and becomes a different one (or before the game ends—as in a hang-up). We can't get really good at these unless we've done so. If we're concentrating on searching for the appropriate response in our Best Practices (in Klpz or in our mind), we'll not be listening as intently to what the target is saying and how they're saying it. That will reduce our Appointment Ratio of conversations to appointments.

But like I said, not everything needs to be memorized. Enter the teleprompter analogy (thanks to Bob Howard, founder of Contact Science, for the idea).

One area that we can apply the teleprompter approach to is voice mails. Because we don't have to worry about the target responding to us, we don't need to worry about splitting our attention and be listening to what they are saying. Also, when using *The Formula's* approach, we'll generally leave a slightly different voice mail on each call in the Cycle, which means that depending on the number of steps in our standard Cycle, there can be a lot of memorization. Once we've familiarized ourselves with each of the messages, it is okay to have voice mail script in front of us in Klpz or printed on our desk to remind us of what the appropriate message will be.

Another area where the teleprompter approach works is in responses to direct questions that might require specificity and/or a lot of detail. Those can actually be *read* like a newscaster does off of their teleprompter. Once we're familiar with the content and have practiced it a few times (and yes, newscasters do read through their material before they go on the air), we can make it sound conversational, and that is the key.

The last area where the teleprompter approach can be applied is in the area of secondary *Bridge Questions*™. *Bridge Questions* are the key to the ball game when attempting to convert a negative response into an appointment. When someone does throw us something different than the predictable negative responses we're traditionally prepared for, having our list of *Bridge Questions* at the ready to resort to and read if necessary can work. Of course, that also assumes we've got a written set of Best Practices to begin with!

Summary—we must have our Best Practices written out. Memorize the opening to limit the responses we'll get and then select the parts of the process that open themselves up to the use of the teleprompter approach and memorize everything else.

WHAT DOES THE ELVIS IMPERSONATOR AND COLD CALLING HAVE IN COMMON? PRACTICE, PRACTICE, PRACTICE

Are you a short cut person? Do you read a book, listen to a CD or watch a DVD and expect the new knowledge to just somehow magically become a part of what you do and how you do it?

Here's an e-mail we received from one of our Prospector's Academy™ attendees that addresses what's necessary to become a success better than I could have ever said it. He set more than twenty Initial Appointments during the two week academy he attended which set a record! Thanks to Steve for letting us share this with you.

"Dear Nancy, Bob & Barry: I did so want to be with you guys today (academy wrap-up session) but my wife had a Summit meeting and they paid my way, so I went. It wasn't all R&R, though. While here I installed a Lexmark copier that I had sold to First Financial Bank.

When through, I went to Chili's and while there, a customer returned one of my voice mails. He wanted to set up an appointment. You should have seen me scrounging for napkins to write on. It made me feel good.

When I met up with my wife, she and her organization were at an Elvis Concert. I was invited so I joined them. This guy didn't physically look like Elvis. He didn't have too. He talked, walked, winked, blinked, and smiled just like Elvis.

I told my wife's organization later at *Outback* that this guy just didn't wake up last week and say, "I think I want to be Elvis."

He watched Elvis movies and concerts. He listened to Elvis songs. He watched how Elvis would talk, walk, wink, and blink. He studied Elvis' mannerisms, the way he spoke, the way he accented his words and phrases. He would go to bed and see Elvis movies--he would go to sleep and dream Elvis concerts.

Then he stood in front of a mirror and got behind a microphone and practiced—and practiced—and practiced—and practiced—until one day, he woke up and he was Elvis.

The same goes for us—more that anything, I want to be a *Great* Solutions Provider. It's not going to happen over night—So, I'm going to study the way you guys talk, walk, wink, and blink. I'm going to study your mannerisms, the way you guys speak, the way you accent your words and phrases. I'm going to watch DVDs and listen to CDs. I'm going to go to bed and hear conditioned responses (negative responses). I'm going to go to sleep and dream *Bridge Questions*[6]. Then one day... I'm going to wake up... and be a *Great* Solutions Provider.

I want to thank you again, Nancy, for yours, Bob's and Barry's hard work and dedication. It will not be forgotten...and will always be appreciated."

Steve Splawn
Solutions Provider (in training)
El Dorado Printing/Discount Imaging

SELLING *RIGHT NOW,* VERSUS ASKING FOR AN APPOINTMENT WHEN COLD CALLING.

This topic comes up a lot in our appointment-making workshops. Once we get a target on the phone, should we be trying to sell them right then and there, or should we be asking for an appointment? Here's our philosophy.

My answer to this and almost all questions we receive during our workshops begins with this basic premise: Nothing works all of the time. However, I'm all about increasing my odds of success and reducing risk. So, when we cold call someone, remember that we are interrupting them from doing something, so in most cases, they don't even *want* to talk to us. Secondly, remember that according to the surveys we've conducted, less than 5 percent of our targets think they are *in the market* for what we're selling when we call them, so they don't think they *need* to talk to us, either.

What those two things mean on a cold call is that we've got a very short period of time to get what we want, so it's best to keep it simple and basic. An appointment doesn't commit them to anything beyond a few minutes of their time. Even if we are selling entirely over the phone, I recommend that we ask for an appointment to do that.

Here are some more quick reasons to do it that way:

- If we get into too many selling conversations when making cold calls (elongating the average length of our calls), most of us sales professionals run out of time to make the required number of calls to make our goals--increasing the risk of not hitting those goals.

- People will open up less to us on the phone than they will in person--meaning we'll miss some percentage of opportunities because people won't be forthright with us--thereby reducing our closing ratio.

- We will tend to feel rushed and therefore more apt to *product dump* on the target hoping we can hit a hot button before they decide this isn't for them; when what we really want (and need) to do is to ask questions to understand how to properly present our solution in their terms.

- When someone grants us an appointment, they generally will stay committed to the time they committed for the meeting--increasing our odds of success.

TO QUALIFY OR NOT, THAT IS THE QUESTION!

On a cold call, should we qualify when we've got someone on the phone?

We're asked consistently, "How much qualifying is appropriate on a cold call?"

Here are our thoughts on the matter:

- The key point to understand is this. People will open up to us more in a face-to-face meeting than they will over the phone, so let's not qualify ourselves out of a sale while trying to set the appointment over the phone. There is no trust or credibility yet built on a cold call. We may still be lied to on the phone if the reason for the question is viewed as entirely selfish. "How many widgets a year do you think you buy a year, Mr. Target?" It's pretty easy to get rid of us if they know we're looking for a large number, right?

- Do we sell to a very broad audience or is it difficult to find our targets? The harder it is to find them, or the fewer there are of them, the less qualifying I might be inclined to do over the phone as I can't afford to miss any opportunities.

- The larger our territory is from a geographic perspective, the more qualifying is appropriate. No sense wasting our time getting there and back.

- If we sell into large organizations, can we find out information on an Initial Appointment that would help us penetrate further into the target? If so, why not go on the appointment? It's getting in the door that can sometimes be the greater challenge.

- Remember, our cold call targets don't think they need us when we call. Add to that the fact we're interrupting them, and we've got a very good set of reasons to keep our calls short. If we're using the concepts we teach in

The Formula, our target should have developed a good understanding of the value of seeing us by the end of the call. Therefore, it is entirely appropriate to ask one or two key qualifying questions after we've gotten their agreement to meet with us.

To accomplish that, we like use the following language after they agree to the appointment: "To help me be better prepared for our meeting, do you mind if I ask you a *couple* of *quick* questions?" This approach won't irritate the target as much than if they think we're going to get into a long drawn out conversation. That's why we're telling them upfront we'll be quick and it will help us make the meeting more productive.

- We must be careful how we ask our questions. This actually happened to me. Since we generally are looking for larger sales forces, one of my favorite qualification questions is to ask how many sales professionals they have. In one instance, the number I heard was smaller than I wanted, but it was with the new indoor arena here in Dallas, so I wanted to go anyway. Turned out that this guy was able to hook me up with several related sales forces that also sold into the arena. His team was small. I've since rephrased that question!

SHOULD WE CALL OUR TARGETS BY THEIR FIRST NAME OR BY THEIR LAST NAME WHEN PLACING COLD CALLS?

I'm often asked when placing a cold call, whether I recommend addressing our target by their first name or by their last name. Here's what we think. It depends!

Seriously though, we have two thoughts on the topic. We would recommend calling the person by their first name under most circumstances. Our reasoning is that if we don't start out that way, once we get into the buying cycle with them, we are at their mercy regarding if it is okay to call them by their first name. If they do not grant us permission, we must either ask if we can (which can be awkward) or we are at a power disadvantage during any negotiation that occurs during the Buying Cycle. If you doubt that, think back on someone you consider an elder and call by their sir name, yet they call you by your given name. Do you feel that they regard you as an equal?

The second thought is all about age and/or experience, the level into which we're calling and comfort level. If we happen to be a young, new sales person (or particularly young sounding over the phone), and we're calling very high, its okay in our book if we address our target by their last name.

But when making the decision for yourself, do what is most comfortable. If you've been brought up calling older adults by their surname your whole life, then go for it. Just make the calls!

WHAT IS THE BEST WAY TO STATE OUR VALUE PROPOSITION ON A COLD CALL?

Or, what is the difference between stating what we can do for our target versus what we've done for others like them?

Most of us define our value proposition as something we can do for the person we're calling. Most people think that would be the best and most logical way to approach it, but there is a better way.

Our surveys indicate that less than 5 percent of our universe of targets thinks they are actually in the market for what we're selling when we call. (Most of our clients tell us it is less than that, by the way.) So why do we think telling someone that we can save them money or that our widgets can increase their productivity will make them want to talk to us? The answer is simple: that's the way we've been taught.

In our workshops we see scripts all the time that generally describe the value of the caller's offer as something they can do for the person they're calling. This doesn't resonate with the target often enough because of two reasons. First is the aforementioned reality that they really don't think they have a problem, and since they're busy, they don't want to take the time to look at a better widget. Second is that many times we callers will also be making a presumptuous statement about how we can help them do what they are doing better without knowing the first thing about how the target is doing it today.

Think about that for a second. How in the world do we know we can help you set first appointments more effectively and efficiently when I first cold call you? You may be better at it than I am. Better yet, you may not have to do it at all, so you don't even do what I sell. That presumption is what turns people off to us cold calling sales professionals. It is actually insulting.

Here's a better way to take our same basic value proposition and reword it to take advantage of human nature. Talk about what we've done for someone else. If we can talk about the results of what we've done for others, even better. The reason that works better is that we all think that everyone else, who does what we do, knows something we don't. So, if we appeal to that human insecurity, we'll have better results.

Here's an example of ours: "...the reason I'm specifically calling you today is that our clients have been consistently reporting back an increase in sales resulting from a doubling or better of the number of Initial Appointments their sales teams are setting after adopting our comprehensive approach to appointment-making..."

It's not just me saying my approach is better...our clients are. Give it a try!

WHAT MAKES A GOOD VALUE PROPOSITION?

In an earlier blog, I talked about how to deliver the value proposition in a way that will be accepted more often than the most common way we see it delivered today. Here's some food for thought on how to actually define our value proposition into a powerful message.

Take a moment (okay, it will take more than a moment, but it will be worth the effort), and write down every challenge our customers have told us that our solution addresses. Then write down each feature our solution delivers and the corresponding benefit(s) our customers tell us they derive from each of those features.

Once we've gone through that exercise, we can pick the most powerful and most quantitative and place this in the *reason for calling today* portion of our script. We just need to remember to phrase it in terms of what our customers are telling us about their results, not our opinion.

IS MY APPOINTMENT-SETTING SCRIPT TOO LONG?

This one is an easy one. If we think it is, it is.

Okay, here's a little more on the topic. Our introduction (of ourselves) includes what we like to call, a seven second commercial. We chose that name for a reason—to remind us that it should be very short.

One of the reasons we suggest starting the purpose for the call with, "The reason I was specifically calling you today is...," is just in case we are a little long, we're signaling to the target that we're getting right to the point. Most will let us continue.

The operative question to ask ourselves is, "Do *we* think it is too long?" Are we getting nervous while continuing to talk? If we are, it's too long.

WHY EVEN OUR BEST VALUE PROPOSITION DOESN'T WORK ON AN APPOINTMENT-SETTING CALL.

Okay, maybe the title is a bit misleading, but I wanted to get your attention regarding one of the subtleties of the appointment-setting process. It *is* our value propositions that are the reasons why people agree to meet with us at the end of day. However, it's when and how we use those value propositions that make the difference between success and failure. The why:

There are two *ground rules* our targets play by when we make cold calls. They are:

1. Less than 5 percent of our universe of targets thinks they are *in the market* when we call them so they don't believe they *need* what we're selling when we call;

2. We are interrupting the target from doing something when we call, so they don't *want* to talk with us.

The Result:

When we tell them all about how the benefits of our value proposition can help them, it falls on deaf ears. They don't care–yet, so it really doesn't matter a whole lot if that we say. That's why even our best value proposition doesn't work, at least to begin with.

We've got to get them past, what we call, their *conditioned knee jerk response* (negative response) and into a short, open-minded conversation before our value proposition will be considered. Here's how *The Formula* approaches that:

1. First we apply a transition from their response to our counter. This transition is based on neuro-linguistic programming concepts of how the brain works. Some of us who have been selling for a while, recognize it as the old feel, felt, found technique. We're basically going to tell them, "It's okay you feel that way. Many of my customers felt that way—until they heard how someone else in their situation was able to—(insert our value proposition here)"

2. Then we ask a Bridge Question™[7] – the key to the ballgame. Bridge questions begin with phrases like, "I'm just curious…" By getting them to answer this question,

we get them to open their mind a little to our application of logic through our counter.

These two steps are how we begin to get our targets to stop thinking about how to get us off the phone and into a short conversation that provides us the opportunity to share our value proposition with them and begin to explore how that might apply to them.

Those that use this process say that it makes them feel much more professional in how they deal with the negative responses they hear.

WHAT'S YOUR FAVORITE RADIO STATION?

How to get that value proposition into our opening script.

Are you an easy listening, classical, hard rock, soft rock, or rap music fan? Let me share with you my favorite. It's WII FM. It's very difficult to find on the radio dial for some reason, although it's playing in every market in the country. I don't care if we're in Chicago, Miami or Gun Barrel City (that's in Texas if you hadn't guessed). It plays whatever we want to hear. As a matter of fact, that's the whole point of WII FM. You see, WII FM stands for *What's in it for me?*

Cute—but where's the tie in to sales and appointment-setting? Simple: Too many of us, when writing our value proposition statements that we use in our cold calling scripts (you are using a script, I hope) concentrate on the value of what we sell from our (the seller's) perspective even though we *think* it is from the potential customer's perspective.

I recommend that we all take some time and go back to some of our current customers and ask them what *they* think is the overall value they derived from doing business with us. Notice that I didn't limit what value they thought your product or service brought to them. By asking a much broader question, we might get a totally different answer regarding why they do business with us.

Once we get a consistent answer that we'd like to talk to our targets about, we build that into the purpose for the call portion of our script, but do it in the following way. We don't just tell them we'd like to meet with them to tell them about the great benefit we can deliver to them. We tell them that we'd like to share with them what our customers are telling us about the impact on their business *they believe* we delivered. If we can make it quantifiable, it becomes even more powerful. i.e.—they told us we helped them increase their profits by 10 percent, cut waste by 23 percent, or doubled the number of Initial Appointments set (I couldn't resist!).

It is a subtle difference, but it gives us third party credibility (from our customers) and it piques their curiosity a bit, particularly if it is something about what one of their competitors, customers, or suppliers is doing (as curiosity killed the cat, right?). Otherwise, we're just another peddler who is paid to say good things about our own product or service. You believe everything sales professionals tell you about *their* products, right?

So let's give ourselves an edge and let our customers say it for us.

THE REASON FOR THE MEETING DOESN'T NEED TO BE EXACT.

I've got a ton of solutions. How do I choose which one to mention?

When creating a *reason for the call* in a cold calling script, many of our Coldcalling101 students are concerned about making sure that they've picked exactly the right one for this particular target. This can be a significant challenge if we've got a lot of solutions to choose from. Here's a tip to help to choose.

Choose the one (reason for the call) that will provide the easiest path to the Initial Appointment, *not necessarily what is sold most often*. We can all tell stories of how we helped customers when they originally didn't think we could. As a matter of fact, the one we choose to lead with could very well be the product we sell the least often.

Remember, the goal of the opening approach is to get a conversation going that allows us the chance to get the Initial Appointment. It really doesn't make any difference what the particular topic is.

Here's another thought that is actually counter-intuitive. Sometimes when our target really doesn't need or want what we open with, they let their guard down a bit because they really believe the pressure is off when you tell them that's okay (see blog entitled *Why even our best value proposition doesn't work on an appointment-setting call*).

When we now bridge to another one of our offerings using one of our *Bridge Questions,* we're likely to get into that conversation we want.

Remember, when they agree to the Initial Appointment, they've agreed to another conversation with us in which we can explore their situation in greater depth, not to purchase what you lead with. Just don't abuse it.

WHY HEARING A DIRECT QUESTION AS THE FIRST RESPONSE FROM OUR TARGETS IS A REALLY GOOD THING—AND TWO TECHNIQUES TO MAKE THAT HAPPEN.

What we all *want* the initial response to our request for an appointment to be is a yes, right? Since that just isn't going to happen very often, what's the next best thing? The answer is, getting a direct question as the initial response.

Why is that? The answer is quite elementary, my dear Watson! It begins a conversation that provides us the ability to apply our skills to get the appointment. It also provides us the platform to build value in the reason they should grant us the appointment. Remember, we've purposely keep our opening *reason for the call* short.

There are two ways to accomplish getting a question in return to our opening approach.

1. Make a *very bold statement* about the results others have experienced using our solution. That gets our target to ask us how we're able to accomplish that. For instance, ours is, "…our clients have been consistently reporting back an increase in sales resulting from a doubling or better of the number of Initial Appointments their sales teams are setting after adopting our comprehensive approach to appointment-making."

2. Be purposefully vague which almost demands a response asking us to explain what we mean.

In either approach, the result is that it gets us into a conversation where we can apply a logical reason for why they should meet with us. Prior to that, it's just us talking and them thinking about how to get us off the phone; and logical arguments just don't work in that environment.

WHY ASKING FOR "…*JUST TEN MINUTES*," ON A COLD CALL PUTS US ON THE DEFENSIVE.

Many times sales people fall back to the position of asking for *just ten minutes* when a target first says no to an appointment request (or even starting with a request for that). That puts us in a very defensive position when we arrive for the appointment.

The objective of most Initial Appointments is for both parties to determine whether it makes sense to enter into a buying cycle or not. If less than 5 percent of our universe of targets thinks they are in the market for what we're selling when we call, we put ourselves at a distinctive disadvantage in telling someone we'll only take ten minutes of their time.

What happens when we take this approach is that we feel pressured when we show up because we're not really sure whether they'll limit us to the ten minutes or not, so we just *product dump* right from the beginning, hoping that the target will hear something that they want to hear more about and extend the visit or grant us another. As a matter of fact, that's what most sales professionals tell us they're really hoping for when they use this approach.

There are two most likely outcomes for a call like this:

1. They'll focus in on something we say during our *product dump* that allows them to quickly come to a negative conclusion about what we are offering that coincides with their belief system before we get a chance to explore how that particular feature might be applied in their environment. "Oh yeah, that's what you're selling. We've got that covered. Thanks for coming by." If it's an incorrect conclusion, we're pretty much cooked; or

2. Our ability to get back into the normal sequence of determining buying motivations is so out of sequence that it is truly difficult to get back to it.

The result of situation number one is that we've wasted a lot of time driving over to their offices, at best. At worst, we've blown an opportunity for a sale.

In situation number two, when it comes time to close, we wind up presenting some kind of proposal based solely on price without understanding what the benefits to the Prospect really are. Our closing ratios suffer and since we only have a certain amount of selling time provided to us by the big guy upstairs, we're doubly wasting our time.

If we really believe we've got something of value, then we need to learn how to handle the, "No," we'll hear and get an appropriate amount of time to conduct an Initial Appointment. Remember, our goal is not the Initial Appointment, it is a sale.

By the way, when selling solutions of significant value to executives, most will assume it is an hour meeting. When we're uncomfortable with how much time we've got, ask when the meeting begins.

WHEN MAKING COLD CALLS, SOME OF US BEGIN WITH, "HOW ARE YOU TODAY?" WHY IS THAT A BAD THING?

As soon as we tell them our name and company (and we should do that), our target knows this is a cold call. They don't recognize our name or our company (unless we work for a company everyone recognizes) so what else could it be? A call to tell them we've found a sizable credit in their name at our company?

One of the precepts of *The Formula* is to always be honest and sincere with people. I don't know about you, but as soon as a cold caller asks me how I'm doing, my defenses go up and I actually find myself irritated. I *know* they don't give a hoot as to how I'm doing. Do you *really* care how they're doing today?

55 percent of communication occurs through non-verbal manners such as facial expressions and body language. Over the phone, that capability is not available to us. Only 7 percent occurs through the words we use. That means that the most effective communication available to us (38 percent) is through tonality. Don't blow it by asking questions that come across as insincere no matter how we deliver it.

If we really want to ask a question early on to get them involved in the conversation (although it is not necessary), try this.

After saying hello (using their name), we can introduce ourselves and our company. Then we can ask if they are familiar with our firm. Regardless of whether they say yes or no, we can respond using our seven second commercial which describes our company and what we do *briefly*. The only difference between the yes, they are familiar with us, or no, they are not, is the first few words. If yes, it may sound something like, "Oh well then you're aware that we are one of the largest…most successful…" If they say no, then say, "Well, we're one of the largest…most successful…"

WHAT ARE THREE QUESTIONS WE *DON'T* WANT TO ASK ON AN APPOINTMENT-MAKING CALL?

When making appointment-making calls, many of us use certain questions that actually make our job more difficult.

First of all, let's get one thing straight right up front. We have every right to make the calls we do (assuming we're calling into businesses or consumers not restricted by no call lists), so let's not be apologetic. Instead, we should be projecting strength and confidence when we call.

The Formula is based on the concept that the target we're calling will do anything, including lie to us, to get us off the phone until we get them past their *conditioned knee jerk response* designed to get us off the phone. If that's the case, why would we want to give them *another* opening to make it easier for them to get rid of us?

Here are three questions we hear callers make all the time that head the list of those to avoid:

1. "Do you have a moment?"
   If you believe, as we do, that the targets we're calling don't believe they need us when we call, asking them if *they have a moment* is just giving them a perfect way to get rid of us. Just get right to the point.

2. "How are you today?"
   If you think about it, when we call our friends, this is not the first question we ask; at least not in the fashion most of us ask this question on an appointment-making call. This approach just signals that this is a cold call. Our target doesn't really believe we care (do we really?), so if we're trying to build credibility we're off to a bad start.

3. "Do you mind if I ask?"
   This question is not as big as the first two. If the target is still looking for reasons to get rid of us, why give them another opening? Use the, "I'm just curious," or, "I was

wondering," approach instead, until we get them into an open conversation where we can apply logical reasons for them to meet with us.

Very few of us like to cold call, so why make it harder? Avoid these questions and you'll be more successful!

WHEN LEAVING VOICE MAILS, WE SHOULD ALWAYS SAY OUR PHONE NUMBER S-L-O-W-L-Y AND THEN REPEAT IT.

We've all received voice mails from someone we actually *wanted* to hear from that made us listen to the messages multiple times in order to completely get the phone number, right?

I have a rule for anyone who calls me. If the person leaving me the message says the number so fast that I have to listen to the message more than twice to get it, I give up and delete the message.

This is one of my pet peeves. Have we become a society that is in such a hurry and so self-centered, that we can't take an extra second or two to leave a message that is understandable for the person we're calling? What message (pardon the pun) are we signaling about our concern for this person should they become a customer if we're not empathetic enough to make their job easier while they're still a potential customer?

Saying the number slowly seems to resonate pretty easily, but some of our workshop participants have said, "But Barry, what if I am calling from a land line to a land line? Why do I need to repeat my phone number again? It's going to be clearly recorded." My answer is to ask a question back in return. "Do you ever check your land line messages from your cell phone and have you ever had a number or a word not understandable on one of those messages?"

By the way, when we're calling a customer, a colleague, even a friend who we know has our phone number (somewhere) do we make it difficult on them and not leave our phone number? Remember, we don't always have our phone book with us.

And if you don't happen to be in an altruistic frame of mind, do it for yourself. Why give our targets another reason to not return our calls? Let's agree to always make it easy on those that have to call us back. Let's say our number s-l-o-w-l-y and repeat it.

WHY WE CAN'T TAKE A NON-RESPONSE TO A COLD CALL VOICE MAIL PERSONALLY.

Sales professionals many times get down when their appointment-setting success rate falls. For instance, we tend to take it personally when our targets do not call us back. After all, we have this really great widget that will turn their lives around, right?

The obvious answer is that if someone is going to call us back, it will not be because of our sparkling personality, it will be because of the value of our message. If that's the case, it stands to reason that when they don't call us back, it is also not because they don't like us.

Here's the key to remember; even our happiest *customers* do not always call us back. That's because they don't look upon what we supply as their top priority when we call them. Although we may get a bit nervous when we don't hear from them right away, we don't take the non-responsiveness personally; we just pick up the phone and try again.

Think of that the next time a target isn't returning a call. Smile into your cold calling mirror and try again. Remember there is a cumulative effect to the calls we make if we're leaving well thought out messages, so don't expect them all to be returned but understand there is value in each message we leave regardless of whether it was returned or not.

And oh yeah…don't take it personally either!

THERE'S A NEW REASON TO LEAVE VOICE MAILS.

Here are seven reasons (including this new one) to leave voice mails.

One of the most common push backs we hear in our workshops on *The Formula* is that some believe that voice mails are a waste of time. I've written on this topic before, but let me take a moment and add another reason to leave them.

There are now seven reasons for leaving voice mails as we've just come across another one that is worthy of mention. People who do not have physical gatekeepers are using their voice mail to screen their calls.

Unless they recognize the caller ID, they won't answer the phone. So if we're not leaving voice mails, we're in a Catch-22 situation. They'll not answer our call because they don't recognize our caller ID and they won't call us back because they don't know who called. (Having our caller ID blocked doesn't work either. See blog entitled, *Caller ID and the mystery cold caller*).

The seven reasons to leave a voice mail:

1. Efficiency – Those that do call us back are pre-qualified (at least they are willing to have a conversation).

2. Efficiency - The majority of the time we invest in making a call is up to the moment we would leave a voice mail. Without Klpz, that could be up to about four to five minutes of our time; with Klpz, about a minute-and-a-half. A voice mail shouldn't be longer than twenty to thirty seconds, so why not invest the additional time?

3. Efficiency – Saved time in not making these calls again. I won't bore you with the details, but if I make fifty dials a day and get only 3 percent of my calls returned, that's close to four hours of calling time per year I can use to call others or to do something else. It does add up.

4. Efficiency - Cold calling is partially a numbers game which means that there are some (less than 5 percent) of our universe of targets that are in the market for what we're selling when we call because they do need us. Therefore, some people will call us back because our timing is right;

5. Effectiveness - Marketing pays big money to advertise our brand (our message) and we've just reached out to a well defined potential customer and we're not going to leave a voice mail? We've already paid for (in our time to place the call) the majority of our effort, so why wouldn't we leverage the effort?

6. Effectiveness - Advertisers say it takes an average of seven to nine touches just to get someone to remember our name.

7. Effectiveness and Efficiency - People use their voice mail to screen calls so if they don't recognize our caller ID (or if we've blocked it), they won't answer the call anyway... ever.

In summary, start leaving voice mails using the concepts of *The Formula*. We'll get more appointments and sales without much of an increase in time or effort.

GATEKEEPERS CAN BE OUR FRIEND.

How to give them reasons to help us. Here are seven suggestions for making the gatekeeper our friend.

Contrary to what most sales professionals think, a gatekeeper's number one responsibility is not to keep us out! Their number one responsibility is to protect and support their boss. On the surface we might think that includes a line in their job description that does say *keep sales people out*, but their real job is to help their boss be successful. In the right circumstances we can help them do that. Since more people (including us) want more of the bosses' time than there is time available, good gatekeepers are invaluable in helping their boss sort through what can actually help them do their job better and what won't or can't.

So what's the moral of the story? We should be thinking about how to help the gatekeeper understand how we can help their boss do their job better. Now I'm also not naïve enough to think that all gatekeepers are created equal, and as I've said before, nothing works all the time, but here are seven rules for working with the best of them:

1. Don't ever lie to trick a gatekeeper to get through to their boss. We may get the first meeting set up, but if the gatekeeper and the boss compare notes--and do we really think they won't? When they do, we're toast. Even if we get to keep the meeting, our trust factor is gone, so we might go merrily along in a buying cycle only to lose the sale at the end when they begin to weigh all of the criteria of doing business with us; .

2. As a rule of thumb, always ask to be put through to voice mail of the person we're calling the first and second time so that we can leave our own message. That way it won't get filtered and restated by the gatekeeper unless necessary. We never know what people take from what we say. (Remember the kid's game of telephone?)

3. Use our standard voice mail message if we must leave a message with the gatekeeper and use the concept of *Pattern Interruption* to keep the gatekeeper from deep drilling us on the reason for the call;

4. Make their job easier and more pleasant, so get to know them. Be one of the people that light up their day and treat them like *they* are the potential customer. We may very well have to sell them on the value we'll bring to their boss before we get to their boss;

5. Always make sure to get their name and make a note of it for future calls;

6. On the third attempt, we should be on a first name basis by now, so ask for their help instead of asking for voice mail or just leaving another message with the gatekeeper. Ask them what they think is the best way to get five minutes of their bosses' time to set an appointment. They will either tell us how to do that (best time to call, send an e-mail, they'll set it up for us, etc.); or they'll tell us we'll not be getting by them.

   One way or the other, we'll know how to get through to their boss; with their help, or calling when they are not there.

7. The really good ones may really grill us as to what the benefit to their boss would be. If they do, simply use the same approach we'd use with their boss unless there is a way we can appeal to their own personal motivations for their boss to listen to our message. (See blog entitled, *How to get the gatekeeper personally engaged.*)

So what do we do if the gatekeeper tells us they will take a message? I call this technique the concept of *Pattern Interruption*.

If we look at one of those old fashioned *While You Were Out* pads, they all use the same order of blanks on the form:

- Date
- Caller's Name
- Caller's Company

- Caller's Phone No.
- *Reason for the Call*

Good gatekeepers want to know what the reason for the call as we discussed a moment ago. Here is a way to reduce the risk of them quizzing us too much on that topic.

First of all, use our normal message just like we would on a voice mail. But here's the trick. Use the concept of *Pattern Interruption* when we recite our information and end up with our phone number being the last thing we tell them.

The reason is that it interrupts their general pattern of thought as the last field is generally the *reason for the call* which triggers the *interrogation.*

Here's the new order:

- Date
- Caller's Name
- Caller's Company
- *Reason for the Call*
- Caller's Phone No.

If the gatekeeper is busy or not really good at their job, they more often than not won't come back and ask us more about the reason for the call again. If they're really good, they will still ask. If they do, then tell them exactly why you're calling. As a matter of fact, just use the same approach we'd use on the boss as if he or she were the person we want to meet with.

HOW TO GET A GATEKEEPER PERSONALLY ENGAGED AND HELPING US.

Do we offer anything that a gatekeeper would personally benefit from if their boss were to buy? If so, make sure the gatekeeper understands that benefit.

We have a client that offers employee benefits. One of their advantages is that they can help stem the tide of decreasing benefits in employee benefit programs caused by increasing costs.

We helped them develop a gatekeeper strategy that appeals to their individual (selfish) concerns in addition to their professional concerns. Instead of entirely appealing to the bosses' issues from the business perspective only, they now subtly talk about how this would impact the gatekeeper's own employee benefits from a personal perspective. When we couple that with the value to the business (the bosses' concern), we're getting pretty good traction with the gatekeeper.

Think about it. If you can play both cards, do it!

HOW TO FIND SOMEONE WITHIN THE TARGET COMPANY TO HELP US GAIN IMPORTANT INFORMATION ABOUT THE PERSON WE NEED TO MEET WITH.

Many times acquired lists have little in terms of the information that would be helpful to us on a cold call. So where do we go to get this information prior to placing the first call to our target name?

I was reading a blog response this week by a cold caller lamenting that targets she's calling today don't seem to be willing to take a moment and talk with us cold callers, even to learn enough from us to determine whether we've got something to offer them or not.

I answered her response with four thoughts on the topic:

1. It's going to get worse. The economy is forcing lay-offs in many companies which will force people to take on even more responsibilities. That means they'll have even less

desire to speak with us when we call, so we better have a compelling *Bridge Question*[8] to get them to stop thinking about how to get us off the phone and into that open-minded conversation we want.

2. More and more people are using voice mail to screen incoming calls so our voice mails better be very compelling. Don't wing it.

3. Call first into the sales department and get a sales professional from their company to help us with a little background information such as who might be the correct person to talk with, etc. Just don't abuse the fact that most of us sales people are likely to be willing to help a fellow sales person. They're busy as well.

4. As a Best Practice, when we start dialing the phone to make appointment-making calls, we'll be more effective if we keep our Call Blocks dedicated to setting appointments. Do that information gathering at a different time. We are more effective when we get rolling, repeating our script, etc. Interrupting that flow with information gathering calls loses that benefit.

ARE THERE REALLY GAZILLIONS OF *CONDITIONED KNEE JERK RESPONSES* (NEGATIVE RESPONSES) OUR TARGETS USE ON US ON AN APPOINTMENT-MAKING CALL?

My wife, Nancy, and I love to hike in the mountains and a while back we were in Sedona, Arizona doing just that. (It's beautiful, by the way if you like rocks; many, many rocks. They even have mountains named as rocks like Red Rock and Cathedral Rock.) Anyway, as we were hiking up this one trail, I stepped on a fairly smooth rock and my boot lost a little traction, causing me to slip. Being a conscientious hiker, I proceeded to kick it off the path after regaining my balance as I certainly didn't want someone else to have the same experience.

But as I did it, I noticed that there were hundreds; no make that gazillions more of them, so I quickly gave up on my crusade to make hiking through Sedona safe for everyone.

So what does this have to do with appointment-setting, you ask? Great question, and thanks for asking! Many times in our workshops on appointment-setting, we're told by our intrepid appointment setters that it is just impossible to prepare for every potential negative response that can occur when making those calls. Those pesky targets seem to have gazillions of them. Like that tie in? Anyway, for some unknown reason, that usually happens right after I assign a little exercise asking them to prepare a list of the most common ones they hear.

While there is some truth to the fact that I am still surprised by a new one from time to time, the good news is that there are really only four categories of what we like to call conditioned knee jerk responses. (Remember Pavlov and his dog?) As a matter of fact, we all have our favorite response to get that caller off the phone when we're cold called. The bad news, of course, is that several of them come in multiple flavors. But we can develop a common approach to each category when countering them. That means that we only have to identify which category they fall into order to handle them effectively. Here are the categories:

- Already got what you sell
- Don't need what you sell
- I'm really busy right now
- Send me some information

But there's even more good news! In our experience, most sales professionals only hear one or, at worst, two on a consistent basis, if-they are consistently delivering the same message in the reason for the call time after time.

Here's some suggested homework to figure out what you hear.

1. Make sure the opening script is consistent; then

2. Track the conditioned knee jerk responses you hear when talking to the person you want the appointment with.

Once you've done that, develop how you'll handle the top one or two. That will have a significant and immediate impact on your success. Once you've got the biggest ones handled and working, address the others.

THERE IS A FIFTH TYPE OF RESPONSE WE GET ON AN APPOINTMENT-MAKING CALL—THE DIRECT QUESTION.

Here are two rules for handling those questions.

Questions received on a cold call are a *very good thing!* However, we must adequately answer those questions if we expect to have a shot at gaining an appointment.

When making cold calls (or any kind of appointment-making call) one of the *predictable responses* many consistently receive comes in the form of questions. Depending on who we are calling, and what we are selling, the questions will vary, but almost everyone receives some consistent set of questions from time to time.

First, there are three reasons to be prepared to answer them and do it effectively:

1. Each of us only has so many hours a day to invest in our business (and set appointments with). If we fail at handling a particular question we've heard before because we've not thought through how to answer, it is not very effective use of our time, is it? As a matter of fact, is was a flat waste of time to make the call in the first place.

2. We must answer questions we receive in the selling process in order to earn the right to ask our own. Dr. Robert Cialdini, in his CD *Influence*, (www.influenceatwork. com) calls this the Principle of Reciprocity. Why would

a stranger be willing to answer our questions if we refuse to answer *their* very first question adequately?

3. Using the techniques we teach in ***The Formula***, we will immediately get into a short conversation which will provide us with the ability to build a little value for the reason they should meet with us.

Take a moment right now (before you forget it) and write down the top three questions you receive when placing appointment-making calls. Then make the time to figure out how you will answer each of those in a complete and concise fashion. The test of adequacy is to ask yourself if you were the one being called, was the answer on the mark, or did it leave you feeling the person calling was skirting the question?

The way we'll then redirect and regain control of the conversation is by asking one of our *Bridge Questions*, which gets us into a conversation on a topic *we* want.

HANDLING THE, "HOW MUCH DOES YOUR SOLUTION COST?" QUESTION ON AN APPOINTMENT-MAKING CALL.

In the previous blog, we talked about the fact that we must be prepared to handle the questions we receive on a cold call in order to be efficient. Here's an example of how to handle the toughest of them all—price.

First of all, let's frame the issue. We don't really want to answer this question do we? We're taught not to bring up price until we've created enough value to support it. If we do, we know we'll more than likely be in a battle of *price only* when asking for the order. So our first impulse is not to answer it.

When someone asks me how much our sales training workshops cost, I really can't give them a definitive price because I don't know enough about their situation. Simply saying that doesn't work though, so I try to put it in a ballpark that is fairly large. Doing this accomplishes four things:

1. It answers the question as best as I can with the information I have (basically none);

2. It does weed out those that can't afford our service immediately;

3. According to Dr. Cialdini's Principle of Reciprocity, I've now earned the right to ask this person a question—they almost have to answer it;

4. If I frame the follow-on *conversation* correctly, (using our bridging technique) it gets me into a short conversation that will provide me with a reason why we should get together.

So here's how I do it using a technique we call the *Bridge Question*[10].

"Well, it's difficult to answer without knowing what type of sales training you might be interested in, how many people you'd want trained, and a few other variables, but let me see if I can at least give you a ballpark idea since you asked.

We have a couple of different programs or approaches. At one end of the spectrum is a self-paced, self-guided approach for smaller teams or individuals which start at about $79 per sales professional. At the other end of the spectrum are fully customized and instructor led programs which can run between $350 to over a thousand dollars per sales professional.

I'm just curious, what are some of the challenges your sales teams are having setting appointments today?" (*Bridge Question.*)

What did I just do? I answered their question fairly based on the information I had (none) and immediately asked them a question that regains control of the conversation and gets us in a conversation about what their challenges are (and off the topic of price, I might add).

WHAT TO DO WHEN AN E-MAIL COLD CALL IS RETURNED WITH A, "NOT INTERESTED."

We've spoken previously about the value of the extra *touch point* generated from using e-mail along with voice mail and the phone to set appointments. But what happens when the target responds with a, "No," via e-mail?

The downside of using e-mail to contact targets is that it is sometimes easier to say no to us in an e-mail. Unless this is a really big opportunity, in which we might want to send a customized message back (see below), I would send the target back a version of the *Move on Message* we've spoken of before. (See blog entitled Top Ten Biggest Mistakes Cold Callers Make on the Phone – No. 9.) Something to the effect of, "Thanks for your response. If you don't mind though, I'll call you again in X days to see if the situation has changed at your end. In the meantime, I wish you well in your selling endeavors and thank again for answering my e-mail. Most people do not take the time to do so."

If it is a big opportunity and we don't want to give up yet, we can send them an e-mail back that basically uses the same counter as what we'd use if on the phone. Using the, "Not Interested," response as an example, I would start with the transition sharing with them that it's okay that they feel that way. Many other of my customers felt the same way until they discovered how much of a revenue impact doubling the number of appointments being set would have on their bottom line. I would then ask a Bridge Question that would kind of say something to the effect of, "Ask yourself this question: what would be the result if ...? If the answer to our question prompts some curiosity on how we have helped people accomplish that, please let me know. Otherwise, if you don't mind, I'll contact you again ..."

WHAT DOES A QUARTERBACK'S ABILITY TO READ DEFENSES HAVE IN COMMON WITH COLD CALLING?

Hint: it's all about countering the negative responses we hear.

I called one of my former students the other day to see how she was doing with her new found appointment-making skills and she said that one the biggest benefits she received from our workshop was the ability to quickly *read the defense* so she can audible to the appropriate *play* to counter what's being thrown at her. (You've got to love the analogy!)

What do I mean by that? When we make an appointment-making call, over 90 percent of the time, we'll get what I refer to as a *conditioned knee jerk response* which is designed to get us off the phone as quickly as possible. We all have our favorite. (Think about it. Don't we all use the same one most of the time when we get cold called?) Although they seemingly come in many flavors, they really don't. As a matter of fact, they can be categorized into only four buckets. Our methodology, called *The Formula*, has its own approach to countering each one of them.

When we're in a face-to-face sales call, we have the ability to actually stop and think when someone throws an objection at us because the person we're talking with has already agreed that the conversation is worth their time. Hence, they're willing to give us the time to think. In a phone conversation designed to set an appointment, we don't have that luxury. We've got to be quick on our feet or we'll lose.

So what does this have to do with my client's analogy? Simple: As soon as we ask for the appointment (start to run our play), the target will throw up their favorite Conditioned Knee Jerk response (their defense). The more quickly we can recognize what kind of defense it is (which category of Conditioned Knee Jerk response), the more quickly and smoothly we can audible to the appropriate strategy (we call them counters) and gain the yardage (the appointment) the play was designed for. (Okay, okay, I know I probably took the analogy one step too far...but I couldn't resist!)

Do you know what the most common conditioned knee jerk responses you hear are? Can you categorize them into manageable buckets? If you've heard a particular flavor at least three times and you've haven't developed a way to handle it yet, shame on you.

HOW TO HANDLE THE, "I'M TOO BUSY TO TALK," CONDITIONED RESPONSE.

I was sitting at a business luncheon the other day and we were all telling each other at the table what we did for a living and I mentioned that I was a sales trainer with a focus on appointment-setting. The young woman sitting next to me was in sales and she asked me for a *free* tip.

After passing on the old line of, "Don't bet on the horses," I asked her what objection she heard most often when calling for an appointment. (We call them conditioned responses because people generally use the same one all the time to get us pesky sales professionals off the phone.) She told me, "I don't have time to talk right now." I asked her how she handled that and she said that she politely asked what would be a good time for her to call back.

I told her before I would give her my approach; I wanted to know why she thought the person was being honest with her and that they really didn't have time to talk. It stopped her dead in her tracks. She told me she never thought about it that way, so I asked her what she said when people cold called her. Was she always honest? She laughed and said she always said the same thing, "I'm in good shape on (whatever they were selling)."

"Always?" I asked.

"Pretty much," she answered.

"So what makes you believe everyone else doesn't use their own favorite Conditioned Response just like you do?" Mine is the too busy to talk one she hears most often as well, by the way.

So here's how I told her to handle it next time:

1. "Hey, I totally understand. As a matter of fact the only reason I called today was to set an appointment. How *is* Tuesday at 2:00?" (Assuming that's what we asked for the first time.) We'll more than likely hear them ask us what we're calling about again because they really weren't listening any more once they realized it was a sales call. They were trying to figure out which of their old standby excuses would work the best on us--proving my point that it was a conditioned or knee jerk response.

2. However, sometimes it is true, right? But don't believe it's true until they tell you a second time—*then* it's okay to ask when would be a good time to call back and take your chances. If you can though, pin them down to a specific day and time and call back at that time.

WHEN IS THE BEST TIME TO CALL FOR AN APPOINTMENT?

In my workshops I am constantly asked, "When is the best time to call targets?" I answer that question in three ways.

First is the old answer none of us want to hear, "It depends." But here's what I mean. Every industry, product or service is different. Different levels of buyers are different. And finally, each of us (callers) is different. We've got to figure it out for ourselves by trying all different times and days and keeping track of our results.

Here's an example of the first variable. When I first began my sales training business I thought calling sales managers on Monday mornings would be a total waste of time. After all, don't most sales managers conduct Monday morning sales meetings? Well it turns out that Monday morning is one of my most productive calling times. Why? Because I typically call on VPs, not front line sales managers.

The VPs don't attend those meetings. And since their direct reports are all tied up conducting those meetings, they're pretty accessible.

So how did I figure that out? By applying the second variable which is that there is no *bad* time to make calls. If we've got the time, get on the phone and make some calls. I did that because I had some time open on a few Monday mornings and a pattern began to develop.

The last variable is us. I make my calls first thing in the morning most days. Why? Because the overriding issue for me is that if I don't do them first, I'll find way too many reasons not do them once I get into my day. As these calls are one of the most important things I need to do, I do them first because I know myself!

The bottom line is, do them and track the results until we see a pattern. Then keep recording the results until we determine if something has changed. Nothing in life is as constant as change.

TO CONFIRM OR NOT TO CONFIRM INITIAL APPOINTMENTS.

I'm often asked whether I confirm the Initial Appointments prior to the meeting. Here are the rules I use to determine whether I do or not.

First a few questions to ask ourselves:

1. How far in advance did we set the meeting?

2. Are we confident that we created enough value with the target when we set the appointment for them to look forward to the meeting?

3. Did we send a confirmation with our contact information directly after setting the appointment with our contact information?

If the answer to the first question is a week or less (generally my pattern), I don't worry about it too much for three reasons.

1. First of all, using the techniques we teach in *The Formula*, I've sold enough value during the cold call for the target to be looking forward to the meeting;

2. I've also asked for an e-mail address after setting the appointment so I could send a pre-configured confirming e-mail directly after the call; and

3. I've sent along, with the confirming e-mail, a document or two that provides some third party credibility for the Caponi Performance Group. (A topic for another day.)

One of the most popular appointment-making methodologies on the market is Stephen Schiffman's. He wrote a book called *Cold Calling Techniques (That Really Work!)*. Some of his techniques still work very well. However, his approach is based on quickly getting the appointment with as little conversation as possible and then getting off the phone. If we do that, there is always the danger that the person will use any secondary contact to cancel the meeting, or at least put us through our paces again to resell it. (As I used to subscribe totally to his methods, I can attest to the worry I had when showing up for appointments without confirming.)

The Formula is based on getting people past their initial Conditioned Knee Jerk reaction designed to get us off the phone at any cost, and into a short conversation. When we do that, we have the ability to provide enough value to make them truly look forward to the meeting.

I'm so sure of the fact that I've accomplished making them look forward to the meeting that I immediately ask for their e-mail address (and I *do* want that) so that I can send them the confirming e-mail I mentioned above.

TWO TIPS TO REDUCE THE NEED TO MAKE COLD CALLS.

Very few of us (including me) likes to cold call. Even when we really believe in what we sell and know it helps the people who buy it, hearing, "No," all the time can beat us down. So what to do?

The answer, my friend is blowing in the wind…wait, that's an old song. The answer is in getting more people to raise their hands to signify their interest (marketing's job) and getting more referrals from our current customers, prospects and network (our job). That way the number of cold calls required is reduced. Here are two tips to do that.

1. Referrals—make it easy for people to come up with appropriate names by helping them limit their thought process while trying to conjure up a referral in their mind. Which question is easier for someone to think of a name?
   a. Who do you know that might benefit from my service?; or
   b. My target market is a company that is in the B2B space that has 10 or more sales people. I'm just curious, who are some of the other sales people that are calling on you presently?
2. Get yourself a copy of Dean Lindsay's book, *Cracking the Networking CODE* – you can order one through my website or directly through Amazon.com.

ABOUT THE AUTHOR

Mr. Caponi is the president and founder of Caponi Performance Group, Inc., a sales consulting and training company located in the Dallas, Texas, area.

His company focuses on assisting its clients increase top-line revenue by assisting its sales teams to get in front of more targets in less time. That is accomplished through its brand, ColdCalling101™, which combines the company's own skills methodology or *Art*, called *The Appointment Making Formula™*, along with Klpz, a web-based specialized prospecting application, known as the *Science*, from Contact Science, LLC.

Mr. Caponi brings over twenty-five years of broad management, sales, and sales management experience to his business. His general management experience includes responsibility for a regional property management firm and worldwide P&L responsibility as a general manager for a division of a software company. On the sales side, in addition to a successful career as a salesperson, he has run local, North American, and global sales teams.

His industry experience includes computer hardware and software, and telecommunications as well as getting his sales start selling life and health insurance. He's worked for multi-billion dollar companies such as Hewlett-Packard and Computer Associates, mid-sized companies such as MetaSolv (now Oracle) of Plano, Texas, as well as his share of start-ups.

Mr. Caponi has closed business in his career that ranged from small deals measured in the thousands of dollars to large deals valued between $30M and $50M. Mr. Caponi has had articles on sales published all across the world in addition to his hometown publications such as the *Dallas Morning News* and the *Dallas Business Journal*.

He can be reached by e-mail at bcaponi@caponipg.com or through his website at www.caponipg.com.

GLOSSARY

Having a common language is important for understanding. In sales, many of the terms that we use are interchangeable, making communication and understanding difficult at best. Have you ever been in a pipeline review session where *prospect* was used to describe someone who had just been identified as potentially a good future customer to pursue—and then, seconds later, the same term was used to describe someone who is almost closed?

Many of the companies that we have helped use different terminology to describe the same things, so here's a glossary of the terms we use in this book:

Art. We use this term to describe the set of skills used to get through to the decision-maker more often and turn more of those conversations into appointments.

Best Practice. We use this term to describe a particular component of Art and/or Science that is adopted by the organization as the de facto way of doing something. Examples of Best Practices are target acquisition approaches, territory building strategy, Cycle or target pursuit designs, the process we'll use to pursue a target over the life cycle of that target, and the messaging we'll deliver when speaking with the target or should we need to leave a message.

Buying Cycle. We use this term to describe what most call a Sales Cycle. We like our term because it is the Prospect—not us—that controls it, regardless of how we want to kid ourselves.

Call Block. We use this term to describe a block of time set aside to make appointment-setting calls.

Conditioned Knee-Jerk Responses. We use this term to describe how most people respond when they are cold called. The important thing to understand is that this is almost always a reflex action. All of us have our favorite way that we get a sales professional off the phone or away from our front door. Generally, it has nothing to do with reality. Also see negative responses.

Counters. We use this term to describe the specific process we have designed within **The Formula** to address the negative response that we generally receive when we ask for an appointment.

Customer. We use this term for consistency. Some companies use other terms such as client, guest, etc. There is no particular importance to be gleaned from our selection of this term.

Cycle. We use this term to describe the framework we define as an adopted Best Practice for the pursuit of a particular class of targets. It contains the type of attempt to contact (snail mail, e-mail, canvas, or phone call), number of attempts we will make before putting this target away again for some predetermined time, frequency of those attempts, and what that predetermined time is before we begin the Cycle again should we be unable to connect during this Cycle.

Dialogue Bond. Coined by a good friend, Bill Wallace, of Dallas, we use this term to describe the phenomena of almost friendship that occurs after talking with someone numerous times over the phone—even if the two parties have never met. This is one of the reasons why we believe that prospecting has a cumulative effect.

Ideal Pursuit Plan. See *Cycle.*

Initial Appointment. We use this term to define a first meeting with a target (not yet a Prospect) in which we (the target *and* us) will attempt to jointly determine whether they are willing and able to become a Prospect for the particular solution we wish to currently sell to them. It could actually be an existing customer for which we will attempt to up-sell or cross-sell, but more typically is someone that we've never met.

In the market. We use this term to refer to someone who realizes a need or desire to solve a challenge and are actively pursuing a resolution. It is an important concept because when we prospect, surveys show that more than 95 percent of our universe of potential targets do not think that they are in the market when we call them.

Move on Message. The last voice mail message in the Cycle of calls that informs the target this will be the last time we call for a while. It generally elicits the largest number of returned voice mails.

Negative Responses. We use this term to describe the different categories of no that we hear when our targets respond to us when we ask for an Initial Appointment. There are only four categories and they are:
- Already have what you sell
- Don't need what you sell
- Don't have time
- Send me something

(Also see Conditioned Knee-Jerk Response.)

Pattern Interruption. We use this term to describe the unorthodox order that we suggest supplying information to a gatekeeper when they take a message for us. The order we use interrupts the pattern they are used to thinking in and reduces the risk of them asking for a more detailed description of the purpose for the call.

Pipeline Phase of the Selling Process. We believe that there are two distinct components to the selling process. The Pipeline Phase begins generally at the end of the Initial Appointment when we, and the target, agree that it makes sense to enter into a buying cycle. It is at this stage the target becomes a *Prospect.*

Prospect. See Pipeline Phase of the Selling Process and Initial Appointment.

Sales Professional. We use this term to describe what most call the Sales Rep or Account Exec. We believe that sales is a profession—hence our choice of the term.

Selling Ratios

> *Appointment Ratio.* The number of Initial Appointments divided by the number of conversations (with the person we want the appointment with) had attaining those appointments.

> *Conversation Ratio.* The number of conversations divided by the number of dials required to attain those conversations.

> *Close Ratio.* The number of sales closed divided by the number of Initial Appointments. (We realize that some people calculate this by using proposals generated as the

denominator, but we like this definition for a variety of reasons beyond the scope of this book.)

Target. We use this term to describe the entity and/or the person we've defined as being someone that could use and afford our solution. We do use the word Prospect, but only after we've met with them and together, we've agreed that they are willing and able to enter into a typical Buying Cycle.

OTHER RESOURCES

In the Introduction, I referenced two white papers that I have written that can also help you with this topic. In several blogs, I also mentioned a Sales Activity and ROI Calculator. For those and more on ColdCalling101™ and *The Appointment Making Formula™*, visit the following websites. Also look for a follow-up book from me in 2012 that will be a full how-to book.

- Caponi Performance Group, Inc.—www.caponipg.com
- Contact Science, LLC—www.contactscience.com
- Blog—www.coldcalling101.com/blog
- YouTube—www.youtube.com/coldcalling101

Although I do not agree with all of the techniques and approaches in the following resources, there are some very good concepts for specific issues that we can all face, depending on our selling environment. For instance, if you're selling into large companies, take a look at *The Power to Get In*. Michael Boylan suggests calling into multiple entry points and letting each know that you're calling into the others. His theory on that is terrific. If you've got a very finite number of targets to sell to, read *Selling to Vito*. Anthony Parinello addresses upfront work before you pick up the phone.

The only three methodologies I mentioned in the Introduction that I at least somewhat agree with are *Cold Calling Techniques, Knock Your Socks Off Prospecting,* and *Red-Hot Cold Call Selling.* Again, I do not agree with all of their concepts, but overall, I think that they have some great ideas and techniques that you can benefit from.

The first resource on the following list is a pretty interesting one. It is a discussion group on LinkedIn dedicated to this topic. You can find some great questions being asked and read some really different approaches to answering those questions. You can then make up your mind as to what might work in your environment.

Here's the full list of resources on appointment-setting:

- LinkedIn Discussion Group—Best Practices for Telephone Prospecting/Cold Calling
- Stephen Schiffman—*Cold Calling Techniques (That Really Work!)*
- William "Skip" Miller and Ron Zemke—*Knock Your Socks Off Prospecting*
- Paul S. Goldner—*Red-Hot Cold Call Selling*
- Anthony Parinello—*Selling to Vito (the Very Important Top Officer)*
- Michael A. Boylan—*The Power To Get In*

The following two resources have had a great impact on our Art methodology. We provide copies of Dr. Cialdini's *Influence* CD to our Prospector's Academy students since it is one of the best overall selling pieces we've run across. It will help you in all phases of selling—not to mention all of your dealings with people. I have customers tell me all the time that they still carry Robert's CD in their car and listen to it over and over.

Neuro-Linguistic Programming is all about choosing the right words (and avoiding the wrong ones) based on studies of how the mind works. Jim Fortin's workshops are the best.

Lastly, Dorothy Leed's *The 7 Powers of Questions* is not a sales book, but it is the best book on questions I've come across. Her concepts apply to all areas of our lives: selling, family, work, everything. Great book.

The particulars on those resources:

- Dr. Robert Cialdini—Studies of why people have the tendency to comply with the requests of others, www. influenceatwork.com
- Jim Fortin, Neuro-Linguistic Programming research and concepts, www.mindauthority.com
- Dorothy Leeds, *The 7 Powers of Questions*

ENDNOTES

1. (This is the script for a cartoon I saw years ago. My apologies to the author for not properly crediting him/her, but I couldn't find his or her name.)

2. The tool we use is called Klpz, from Contact Science, LLC, located in Memphis, TN

3. See Top Ten Biggest Mistakes Cold Callers Make on the Phone – No. 1

4. See Top Ten Biggest Mistakes Cold Callers Make on the Phone – No. 1

5. See Top Ten Biggest Mistakes Cold Callers Make on the Phone – No. 1

6. See Top Ten Biggest Mistakes Cold Callers Make on the Phone – No. 1

7. See Top Ten Biggest Mistakes Cold Callers Make on the Phone – No. 1

8. See Top Ten Biggest Mistakes Cold Callers Make on the Phone – No. 1

9. See Top Ten Biggest Mistakes Cold Callers Make on the Phone – No. 1

10. See Top Ten Biggest Mistakes Cold Callers Make on the Phone – No. 1